Thucydides' Melian Dialogue

Commentary, Text, and Vocabulary

Paula Debnar

Thucydides' Melian Dialogue
Commentary, Text, and Vocabulary

First Edition

The Greek text is the edition by H. Stuart Jones, published by Oxford University
press in 1902.

ISBN-13: 9780692772362
ISBN-10: 0692772367

Published by Paula Debnar
Cover photo by author

Table of Contents

PREFACE

This commentary is aimed at undergraduates at the advanced intermediate level and above, although the second half of the Dialogue contains passages that even advanced students will find challenging. My hope is that it will also be useful for those in fields outside classics who have studied Greek, but who need guidance through some of Thucydides' knottiest syntax. Opposite each page of Greek I have provided a vocabulary list; however, words used more than eight times in the Dialogue, as well as basic vocabulary most students will have learned before approaching Thucydides' History, are listed in the Core Vocabulary preceding the commentary. These words should be reviewed as soon as possible. The Vocabulary at the back of the book contains both core vocabulary and words that appear on individual pages. Preceding the commentary and text (from the 1902 edition by H. Stuart Jones, with line numbers corresponding to pages of that edition), there is a list of grammatical constructions appearing with some frequency in the Melian Dialogue. These aids are intended as starting points; they do not eliminate the need to consult a Greek lexicon or grammar. At the end of the Introduction I have also provided lists of commentaries that provide notes on the Melian Dialogue and of translations of the History.

It will quickly become apparent that Thucydides' Greek grows increasingly difficult up to about chapter 110, so that some pages contain more grammatical notes and glosses than do earlier passages. As with the vocabulary, the glosses should also be viewed as starting points. In some cases there are other ways to analyze the syntax or render the Greek, and it is necessary to examine the Greek closely to see *how* I arrived at a suggested gloss. Only a few comments address likely problems in the text, where without them it might be difficult to unravel the syntax.

For many years I considered writing a grammatical commentary on the Melian Dialogue; however, it took the encouragement and help of Geoffrey Steadman, who provided templates, text, and initial vocabulary lists, to induce me to undertake this project. His assistance has been invaluable, and I extend to him my warm thanks. As usual, I am also grateful to Mary Bellino, who cast her keen editorial eye over the final text.

Finally, I offer heartfelt thanks to three undergraduate students at Mount Holyoke College, Madeline Ketley ('17), Ruiqi (Lady) Shi ('17), and Kathleen Smith ('18), who "test-drove" the commentary in a course on Thucydides in the fall of 2016. Their astute observations about comments that could be clearer and their ability to identify superfluous notes both improved the commentary and made the final stages of this project especially enjoyable and satisfying.

Paula Debnar
Mount Holyoke College
South Hadley, Massachusetts
pdebnar@mtholyoke.edu

INTRODUCTION

In 416 BCE, fifteen years after the commencement of the war between Athens and Sparta, the Athenians decided to bring under their rule Melos, an island about seventy miles north of Crete. The expedition took place six years into the Peace of Nicias (also called the Peace of 421), which Thucydides claims was no real peace, but simply a lessening of hostilities within a single war lasting from 431 to 404 BCE.[1] The Athenians had sent a force against the island once before in 426 (Thuc. 3.91.1–2), but quickly abandoned their efforts.[2] In 416 they meant business.

According to Thucydides, in an effort to persuade the Melians to submit peacefully, before launching their assault the Athenians sent envoys to the city, who were taken to the city's leaders rather than to the assembly of the people. Since some of the Melians at the conference are referred to as "the few," and since the representatives as a whole appear not to consult the people of Melos, it seems safe to assume that Melos had some form of oligarchic government.[3] More important, however, as emerges from the Dialogue, according to Thucydides political ideologies played little if any role in this episode. Instead, the Athenians' desire to expand their empire drove them to attack the island, and the wish to maintain their freedom and autonomy motivated the Melians' decision to resist.

---

[1] Hereafter all dates are BCE, unless otherwise noted.

[2] Andrewes explains their hasty departure by their need to meet up with troops in Boeotia at a prearranged time. See Gomme et al., *A Historical Commentary on Thucydides,* p. 156 n. 1.

[3] Thucydides is the only source for Melos' oligarchy; see Hornblower ad 5.84.3 in *A Commentary on Thucydides.*

While not the sole private conference in the History, the Melian Dialogue is the only one Thucydides casts in direct speech.[4] Aside from the short exchanges between Archidamus and the Plataeans in Book 2, it is also the only political debate in dialogue form. The form is important.[5] The Athenians claim that the Melians' choice of a private meeting is aimed at preventing them from wielding their rhetorical skills to persuade the people of Melos to relent. That may have been the case. But what the Athenians lose by this restriction, they make up for by assuming control of the exchange, at least to begin with.

At the outset the Athenians establish the terms of the discussion: they themselves will begin and the Melians will respond by immediately raising objections to any point with which they find fault; arguments will be short and limited to what is useful in the present circumstances; there will be no talk of justice. The negotiations, in other words, must focus solely on the Melians' survival. If the Melians stray from these limits, the Athenians warn, they will break off negotiations and commence hostilities. Although the Melians subtly try to broaden the discussion by arguing, for example, that justice itself is useful even to the Athenians, the envoys quickly bring them back to the matter at hand: their survival and the mutual benefit of their surrender. Even the Melians' proposal of neutrality is dismissed as less beneficial to Athens than their subjection. And when the Melians contend that by the conquest of Melos the Athenians will create for themselves more enemies, the Athenians brush aside their warning with a peremptory, "Let us deal with the risk."

---

[4] On Thucydides' claim (1.22) that in some way speeches reflect historical models, see Debnar 2001, 14–20, which provides further bibliography.

[5] Price (2001, 195–204, esp. 198) discusses the relationship of the Melian Dialogue to tragic and philosophical dialogue and attributes its failure as a "mutual investigation" to the irreconcilable differences in worldviews of the interlocutors. See also Wassermann 1947.

Thwarted in all their attempts to follow the rules of the debate, about halfway through the Dialogue (5.100) the Melians conclude, with more than a touch of sarcasm, that if the Athenians work so hard to retain their empire, and their subjects are so keen to rid themselves of Athens' rule, they would be cowards not to resist. From here to the end of the dialogue, the Melians take the lead in the exchange, emphasizing honor, piety, hope, divine fortune, and trust in Sparta, while the Athenians are forced to respond—and do so at greater length.[6] They point out the futility of the Melians' trust in the gods and of their faith in the Spartans. They are right, of course, to insist that submission is the Melians' best chance for survival. But it is difficult not to sympathize with the Melians' dilemma and their desire to resist.[7]

Along with Pericles' Funeral Oration, the description of the plague in Athens, and the passage on civil strife in Corcyra, the Melian Dialogue ranks as one of the most memorable episodes in the History. As is true of all of these passages, the very power of Thucydides' account makes it vulnerable to being isolated from its immediate context and from the larger webs of narrative and speech woven throughout the History. Context in this case is all the more important if, as has been argued, the complete History would have comprised ten books.[8]

---

[6] See Stahl 2003, 163

[7] Even de Romilly (1979, 290), who focuses on the general nature of imperialism and stresses Thucydides' impartiality, admits that the episode elicits sympathy for the Melians. See also Andrewes at 5.97 (Gomme, et al., *A Historical Commentary on Thucydides*). In contrast, Bosworth (1993) emphasizes the foolishness of the Melians, given their desperate situation; see also Stahl 2003, 159–72, and Gillis 1978. On the difficulty of discerning Thucydides' own opinions of the Athenian Empire, see Hornblower 1987, 171–78.

[8] The History, as it has come down to us, breaks off in the eighth book in 411, seven years before the Spartans finally win the war. On the ten-book structure, see Rawlings 1981, esp. 216–40; he revives the idea that the History would have ended with a dialogue about the fate of Athens, paralleling the earlier one about Melos.

In this case the Melian Dialogue would have appeared at (or very near) the end of the first pentad, punctuating, as it were, the conclusion of the period of the war from its outbreak through the unstable Peace of Nicias. In this position it also would have served as a hinge turning the reader to the final five books, which begin with the Athenians' disastrous Sicilian Expedition and most likely would have ended with the fall of Athens.

Even without a ten-book theory, the themes shared by the Dialogue and the Sicilian Expedition, such as the unrestrained urge to expand imperial power, colonization, kinship ties, and the behavior of victors towards the vanquished—to mention but a few—encourage readers to reflect on the one while reading the other.[9] In particular, the Melians' stubborn resistance to invaders points forward to the defeat of what must have seemed an invincible power when Athens' fleet first set sail to conquer Sicily. So, too, the speech of the Athenian general Nicias, in which he tries to inspire his troops in Sicily with his futile appeals to hope and traditional piety, echoes the Melians' final statements.

The Melian Dialogue looks back in the History as well. The Melians' request to be allowed to remain neutral, friends of both sides but active combatants on behalf of neither, recalls King Archidamus' offer to the Plataeans in Book 2.[10] In 429, at the head of the Peloponnesian League, the Spartan king marched against Plataea. Before laying siege to the city, which was closely allied with Athens, he proposed that the Plataeans remain neutral. Recognizing, however, that they feared retribution from their hostile Theban neighbors once the Peloponnesian

---

[9] See, e.g., Liebeschuetz 1968. Orwin (1994, 118–41) devotes a separate chapter to Melos and Syracuse. Even first-time readers can retrospectively detect some echoes, and, of course, when reading the Melian Dialogue, Thucydides' contemporary audience would have been well aware of the hopes concerning the expedition to Sicily and its fate.

[10] Wasserman 1947.

forces departed, Archidamus proposed that they physically remove themselves from the city, as well as from the war, and hand over all their land and possessions to the Spartans for safekeeping for the duration of the conflict. Thucydides suggests that the Plataeans found the offer attractive. They were prevented from accepting it, however, by their Athenian hegemons, who, despite their claim that they had never abandoned the Plataeans before, failed to come to their aid. Once the city surrendered, following a sham trial all the remaining inhabitants of Plataea were put to death. Now, after fifteen years of war, any offer of neutrality is out of the question.[11] Instead, the Athenian envoys claim that for a sea power such as themselves failure to subject an island like Melos to their rule would be but a sign of weakness and an invitation for others to refuse to submit or to rebel.

The Dialogue also points to Book 2 and Pericles' Funeral Oration, whose ideal Athens, yet to experience the pressures of a long war and repeated attacks of the plague, is said to rule through generosity—by giving rather than by taking (2.40.4).[12] Although Pericles passes over the standard praise of Athens' role in the Persian Wars, his mention of what the Athenians of his own time inherited from their forebears (2.36.2) draws attention to that generation's resistance, against all odds, to Persian aggression—something the Athenian envoys in Sparta in Book 1 explicitly recall before the commencement of the war (1.73.2–5). From this perspective, the Athenians in Melos in Book 5 are, as their enemies liked to portray them, the new Persians against

---

[11] Cogan (1981, 87–93) sees the elimination of any prospect of neutrality as a mark of the transition to the second, more ideological, phase of the war, which heightened fears and left total victory or defeat as the only options.

[12] Connor 1998, 153 n. 33. Price (2001, 143), however, points out that what Pericles describes in 2.40 is still an imbalance in Athens' relation with other cities instead of customary reciprocity.

whom the Melians resist.[13] Moreover, while the Athenians on Melos dismiss the value of appeals to "fine words" like honor, Pericles extols the nobility, heroism, and honor of the Athenians who died in the first year of war as they fought for their city (2.41.5–42)—this at a time when no Greeks thought the Athenians would hold out for more than three years against the Spartan alliance (Thuc. 7.28.3)

There are other echoes.[14] The Melians are not unlike the small number of Spartans in Book 4 who were trapped on the tiny island of Sphacteria but managed to hold out against a huge number of Athenian forces by sneaking in food and supplies (4.26.4–8). The Spartans on the island were betrayed by bad luck, when a fire removed the brush disguising the small size of their forces and emboldened the Athenians to make their final successful assault. The Melians, in contrast, are betrayed from within (as are the Mytilenians in Book 3). Nonetheless, a successful siege was not a certain thing.[15] As the Spartans who sue for peace after the debacle on Sphacteria (4.17–21) remind the Athenians, it is impossible to predict the twists and turns of fortune in war—a lesson the Athenians will learn firsthand in Sicily.[16] Part of the challenge as well as the enjoyment of reading the History is identifying such echoes and foreshadowing, and weighing the similarities of events and arguments against their differences.[17]

---

[13] Crane (1998, esp. 237–57) looks further back to Homer, Hesiod, and Herodotus—in particular to the Athenians' speech on resisting the Persians in Herodotus' *Histories* (8.144)—as well as to values expressed in Greek tragedy. See also Connor 1998, 155–57.

[14] See, e.g., Stahl 2003, esp. 162–66, and Macleod 1983, 52–67.

[15] According to Herodotus (8.112.1–3) the Athenians had abandoned at least one siege, even if in Thucydides they claim never to have abandoned a siege because of fear (5.111.1).

[16] See also the Corinthians at 1.1222.1. On differences between the situations of Sparta and Melos see Bosworth 1993 and Stahl 2013, 159–72.

[17] On this way of approaching Thucydides see Morrison 2006; see also the conclusions of Rood 1998, esp., 286–93.

The Dialogue also poses historical questions.[18] Depending on the date of an inscription recording contributors to Sparta's war efforts,[19] the appearance of Melos on the stone could suggest that the Melians were partisans of Sparta at the time of the Athenians' attack. Different lines of the list, however, seem to have been inscribed at different times. The contribution attributed to Melos could very well come from late in the war and refer to Melians whom Lysander restored to the island after 404—or even represent small contributions from Melians who escaped the slaughter in 416 and were likely to have been resettled by the Spartans.

Conversely, the appearance of Melos on an Athenian inscription recording reassessments of tribute for the year 425/4 (not mentioned in the History) seems to indicate that the Melians had been brought under Athens' rule before 416 and that their absence from the list of actual contributors is evidence of refusal to pay tribute and therefore of rebellion.[20] As Lisa Kallet-Marx has argued, however, one reason Thucydides did not mention the reassessment may have been that it was so ineffective; in her view the inscription was a symbolic expression of the Athenians' confidence, given recent successes, rather than a bonafide list of allies.[21] In effect, it laid claim to the Athenians' right to rule the islands of the Aegean, asserting that Melos *should be*, even if it was not in fact, part of Athens' empire. More important, there is no hint in Thucydides' History that refusal to pay tribute or rebellion was grounds for the attack on Melos.

Neither is there evidence that the Athenians considered the Melians to be enemies of war by virtue of their response to Athenian aggression

---

[18] See Seaman 1997, which provides detailed and convincing arguments about the historical circumstances of the conquest of Melos.

[19] The so-called Spartan War Fund Inscription, *IG* v 1.1 (in Lewis 1981).

[20] *IG* 13 71 = ML 69 in Meiggs and Lewis 1969.

[21] Kallet-Marx 1993, 164–70. See also Meritt et al. 1950, 196.

in the assault in 426. In reference to the earlier attack Thucydides does say that, when the Athenians forced them by devastating their land, the Melians "openly went to war" (ἐς πόλεμον φανερὸν κατέστησαν, 5.94.2).[22] Given that there is no mention of a treaty, does this mean that they were not neutral, but formally at war with Athens in 416? Such a scenario seems both unlikely and overly legalistic.[23] Before the Peloponnesian War began Corinthian and Athenian ships engaged in battle at Corcyra. Nonetheless, after the battle the Athenians assured the Corinthians that they did not view them as "enemies of war," that is, they did not consider Athens to be formally at war with Corinth. Similarly, although in 426 the Melians may have engaged in battle with the Athenian forces ravaging their land, it seems likely that neither side considered the other an enemy of war. Moreover, it was customary for city-states officially at war to restrict communication to exchanges of heralds. There is no evidence in the History, at least, that in 416 either side seemed to have thought this necessary.

It is far more probable that the strategic position of the island, en route from the Peloponnese to Ionia and North Africa, made Melos a likely target for Athenian aggression.[24] Once the island of Thera had submitted, Melos remained the only independent island to speak of in the southern Aegean. The Athenians wanted—and believed they were

---

[22] In his commentary (at 5.84.2) Hornblower takes this as an "indeterminate reference," meaning that it is not clear whether the reference is to 426 or 416. Given, however, that in the second expedition to Melos the Athenians are said to confer *before* harming the Melians' land, the statement seems out of place in 416; moreover, οὖν at 5.84.3 marks a return from 426 to 416.

[23] Similarly Seaman (1997, 389) thinks that ἐς πόλεμον φανερὸν κατέστησαν means "they engaged in acts of open hostility with the Athenians but did not escalate the hostilities to the extent that they invalidated their neutral status."

[24] Seaman (1997, 411) points out the likely connection between the Athenians' first attempt to subdue Melos and the movement the previous year (427) of a Peloponnesian fleet through that part of the Aegean to Ionia.

entitled to—all of them. As Thucydides presents the episode, the Athenians sent an expedition to subdue the Melians because they had the power to accomplish their goal. There is no question of an offense. The Melians themselves assert this point when they claim that they are righteous men taking a stand against men who are unjust (5.104.1). Thucydides leaves the matter at that.

The Melians' belief that the Spartans would come to their aid, primarily because of their kinship and proximity to the Peloponnese, has struck some readers (as it does the Athenian envoys in the History) as remarkably naive and foolish. Thucydides confirms that Melos was a Spartan colony and thus linked by kinship. He also reports that before the attack on Melos the Spartans had, in fact, gone to the aid of other kin—twice in Doris (1.107.2 and 3.92.3); they do so again in 413 when they help the Euesperitae (in North Africa), related by means of their connections to Thera, also a Spartan colony (7.50.2). Clearly, the Spartans felt the tug of kinship ties and sometimes acted on them.

But how much did the Melians know about the Spartans? Their ignorance of Sparta's current circumstances, at least, suggests that they had had little recent commerce with their mother-city. First and foremost, they seem unaware that, based on the Spartans' naval record in the war, they were unlikely to be willing to confront Athens' fleet directly. Nor do the Melians take into account that, even if the Spartans considered sending help, they would have been reluctant to risk breaking the Peace by precipitating a naval battle between Athenian and Peloponnesian forces. Thucydides later reports that the Spartans attributed their bad fortune in the first ten years of the Peloponnesian War to their having failed to live up to the oaths of the Peace of 445 (7.18.2). It is hardly likely that in 416 they would be eager to break another treaty. Instead, the Spartans waited for an open rupture of the Peace by the Athenians in the summer of 414 (6.105.2) to invade Attica and establish a garrison in the deme of Decelea.

Finally, the Melians seem unaware of the Spartans' likely naval weakness. The Spartans were not on good terms with the Corinthians, their main naval ally, and even Corinth's fleet may have been depleted after so many years of war. There is no suggestion in the History, at least, that Sparta or members of its alliance had replaced the ships the Athenians confiscated in 425 at Pylos.[25] Rather, given how few ships they initially send to Sicily, it is possible that in 416 their fleet was greatly diminished. Had the Spartans, that is, been willing to send aid to Melos, it is not clear that they could have.[26]

In sum, neither Thucydides nor other sources provide answers to the historical questions the Melian Dialogue raises.[27] Asking them, however, draws attention to how narrowly the historian circumscribes the issues at the heart of the debate, focusing it on the clash between the Melians' adherence to traditional moral notions and the Athenians' thesis that the strong naturally rule over the weak wherever they can— and that they must.[28] This clash, in barest terms one between custom (νόμος) and nature (φύσις),[29] is reflected in the abstract level at which the arguments are conducted and in the sophisticated rhetoric of the debate.[30] The exchanges abound in both complicated generalizations and abstract noun phrases, like τὰ εἰκότα (*the reasonable*) and τὸ ἀνθρώπειον (*the human,* i.e. *men*). The Athenians rationalize their

---

[25] Seaman 1997 and Debnar forthcoming.

[26] Seaman (1997) suggests the timing of the Athenians' attack on Melos reflects their understanding of these factors.

[27] After reviewing the historical issues Seaman (1997, 409–11), however, concludes that there is no evidence to refute Thucydides' version of the episode. Moreover, as Pouncey (1980, 88) observes, "the narrative is deliberately cleared of all contextual information, any record of grievance or politics attending the event, so that the Athenian action is made to appear a perfectly gratuitous act of aggression."

[28] Crane 1998, 237–93. See also de Romilly 1979, 286–310.

[29] On the Athenians' specious conflation of the two, see Gomez-Lobo 1991.

[30] On the Dialogue's rhetoric see Macleod 1983 and Morrison 2006, esp. 83–94.

exercise of power with the claim that this is how the powerful, including the gods, have always acted and always will. Their lofty warning about the treacherous nature of hope is especially difficult to parse. Slow and careful reading of the exchanges, however, reveals the echoes between assertions and retorts, the clever manipulation of opponents' statements, and the strengths and weaknesses of both sides' positions. In short it reveals the reasons the Athenians and Melians could never reconcile their differences, in speech or in deed. It also shows how in the Melian Dialogue Thucydides creates the greatest tension between the drama of events as they unfold and their general import.[31] In this sense, it is especially useful for Thucydides' intended audience, those who want to know clearly what happened and what will, more or less, happen again in accordance with τὸ ἀνθρώπινον (1.22), "what it means to be human."

---

[31] De Romilly 1979, esp. 297–31.

WORKS CITED

Many of the following (restricted to works in English) also provide good starting points for further study of the Melian Dialogue or of Thucydides in general. Commentaries referred to in the Introduction appear on the next page.

Bosworth, A. B. (1993). "The Humanitarian Aspect of the Melian Dialogue." *JHS* 113: 30–44.

Cogan, M. (1981). *The Human Thing: The Speeches and Principles of Thucydides' History*. Chicago.

Connor, W. R. (1984). *Thucydides*. Princeton.

Crane, G. (1998). *Thucydides and the Ancient Simplicity: The Limits of Political Realism*. Berkeley.

Debnar, P. (forthcoming 2018). "Βραδυτὴς Λακονική: Spartan Slowness in Thucydides' History of the Peloponnesian War," in P. Debnar and A. Powell, eds., *Sparta and Thucydides*. Swansea.

______. 2001. *Speaking the Same Language: Speech and Audience in Thucydides' Spartan Debates*. Ann Arbor.

Gillis, D. (1978). "Murder on Melos," in *Rendiconti: Classe di lettere, scienze morali, e storiche* (Istituto Lombardo: Accademia di Scienze e Lettere), 185–211. Milan.

Gomez-Lobo, A. (1991). "Philosophical Remarks on Thucydides' Melian Dialogue." *Proceedings of the Boston Area Colloquium in Ancient Philosophy*, 5: 181–203. Lanham.

Hornblower, S. (1987). *Thucydides*. London.

Kallet-Marx, L. (1993). *Money, Expense, and Naval Power in Thucydides' History 1–5.24*. Berkeley.

Lewis, D. (1981). *Inscriptiones Graecae*, 3rd ed. Berlin.

Liebeschuetz, W. (1968). "The Structure and Function of the Melian Dialogue." *JHS* 88: 73–77.

Macleod, C. W. (1983). "Form and Meaning in the Melian Dialogue,"
in *Collected Essays*, 52–67. Oxford.

Meiggs, R., and Lewis, D. (1969). *A Selection of Greek Historical
Inscriptions*. Oxford.

Meritt, B., H. Wade-Gery, and M. McGregor (1950). *The Athenian
Tribute Lists,* Vol 3. Cambridge, Mass., and Princeton.

Morrison, J. V. (2006). *Reading Thucydides*. Columbus, Ohio.

Orwin, C. (1994). *The Humanity of Thucydides*. Princeton.

Pouncey, P. (1980). *The Necessities of War: A Study of Thucydides'
Pessimism*. New York.

Price, J. J. (2001). *Thucydides and Internal War*. Cambridge.

Rawlings, H. R., III. (1981). *The Structure of Thucydides' History*.
Princeton.

Romilly, J. de (1979; reprint of 1963). *Thucydides and Athenian
Imperialism*. Trans. P. Thody. New York. Originally published as J.
de Romilly, *Thucydide et l'imperialsime athénien* (Paris, 1963).

Rood, T. (1998). *Thucydides: Narrative and Explanation*. Oxford.

Seaman, M. (1997). "The Athenian Expedition to Melos in 416 B.C."
Historia 46: 385–418.

Stuart Jones, H. ed. (1902). *Thucydidis Historiae*, Vol. 1. Oxford.

Stahl, H.-P. (2003). *Man's Place in History*. Swansea. Translated and
expanded 2nd edition of H.-P. Stahl, *Thukydides: Die Stellung des
Menschen im geschichtlichen Prozess, Zetemata* 40 (Munich, 1966).

Wassermann, F. (1947). "The Melian Dialogue." *TAPA* 78: 18–36.

COMMENTARIES INCLUDING THE MELIAN DIALOGUE

Bloomfield, S. (1843). *The History of the Peloponnesian War by
Thucydides*, Vol. 2. London.

Classen, J., & J. Steup (1892). *Thukydides III.* (3rd ed.). Berlin. (In
German.)

Fowler, H. N. (1890). *Thucydides: Book V.* Boston. (This commentary is based on Classen's.)

Gomme, A. W., A. A. Andrewes, and K. J. Dover (1970). *A Historical Commentary on Thucydides,* Vol 4. Oxford.

Graves, C. E. (1899). *The Fifth Book of Thucydides.* London.

Hornblower, S. (2010). *A Commentary on Thucydides,* Vol. 3. Oxford.

Nagy, B. (2005). *Thucydides Reader: Annotated Passages from Books I–VIII of the Histories.* Newburyport, Mass.

TRANSLATIONS

Most of the suggestions below are in contemporary English. Hobbes' translation remains useful because his seventeenth-century prose often captures the rhetorical effects of Thucydides' Greek.

Blanco, W. (1998). *Thucydides, The Peloponnesian War.* Edited by W. Blanco and J. Roberts. New York.

Hammond, M. (2009). *Thucydides: The Peloponnesian War.* Oxford.

Hobbes, T. (1989). *Thucydides, The Peloponnesian War: The Complete Hobbes Translation.* Commentary by David Green. Chicago.

Lattimore, S. (1998). *Thucydides, The Peloponnesian War.* Indianapolis.

Mynott, J. (2013). *Thucydides: The War of the Peloponnesians and the Athenians.* Cambridge.

Strassler, R., ed. (1998). *The Landmark Thucydides: A Comprehensive Guide to the Peloponnesian War.* New York. (This edition, with a revised version of R. Crawley's 1874 translation, contains useful maps and essays.)

Warner, R. (1972). *Thucydides: The History of the Peloponnesian War.* Edited by M. I. Finley. Baltimore.

CORE VOCABULARY

The following is an alphabetical list of all words that occur more than eight times in the Melian Dialogue (5.84–116), as well as some words that are assumed to be known by the time students reach the intermediate level of Greek at a college or university (based in part on Cheadle's list of 1,000 words in Attic). These words are not included in the commentary and therefore should be reviewed as soon as possible.

ἀγαθός, -ή, -όν: good, brave, capable

ἄγω: to lead, to bring, carry, convey

Ἀθηναῖος, -α, -ον: Athenian, of Athens

αἰεί: always, forever, in every case

ἀκούω: to hear, listen to

ἀλλά: but

ἄλλος, -η, -ο: other, one...another

ἀνήρ, ἀνδρός, ὁ: man, husband

ἄνθρωπος, ὁ: human being

ἄπας, ἄπασα, ἄπαν: every, quite all

ἀπό: from, away from (gen.)

ἀρετή, ἡ: excellence, goodness, virtue

ἄρχω: to begin; rule, be leader of

αὐτός, -ή, -ό: him-, her-, itself; he, she, it; the same

βουλή, ἡ: council, plan, will

βούλομαι: to wish, be willing, desire

γάρ: for, since

γε: at least, at any rate; indeed

γῆ, ἡ: earth, land

γίγνομαι: to come to be, become, be born

γιγνώσκω: to come to know, learn, recognize; to form a judgement, think

δέ: but, and, on the other hand

δεινός, -ή, -όν: terrible; wondrous, clever

δέχομαι: to receive, accept

διά: through (gen.), on account of (acc.)

δίδωμι: to give

δίκαιος, α, ον: just, right, lawful, fair

εἰ: if, whether

εἰμί: to be, exist

εἶπον: (aor.) said, spoke

εἰς (ἐς): into, to, in regard to (acc.)

ἐκ, ἐξ: out of, from (gen.)

ἐλπίς, -ίδος, ἡ: hope, expectation

ἐν: in, on, among (dat.)

ἐπί: near, at (gen.); to (acc.); upon (dat.)

ἔχω: to have, hold; be able; be disposed

ἤδη: already, now, at this time

ἡμεῖς: we

ἤν (ἐάν, εἰ ἄν): if, if ever

ἴσος, -η, -ον: equal to, the same as, like

καί: and, also, even, too

καλέω: to call, summon, invite

καλός, -ή, -όν: beautiful, fair, noble, fine

καλῶς: well; beautifully

κατά: down from (gen.); down (acc.)

κοινός, -ή, -όν: common, ordinary; public

Λακεδαιμόνιος, -α, -ον: Lacedaemonian

λαμβάνω: to take, receive, catch, grasp

λέγω: to say, speak

λείπω: to leave, forsake, abandon

λόγος, ὁ: word, speech, discourse, argument

μέν: on the one hand

μή: not, lest

xxi

Μήλιος, -α, -ον: Melian, from Melos
νῆσος, ἡ: an island
νομίζω: to believe, think, deem
νόμος, ὁ: law, custom
νῦν: now; as it is
ξύμ-μαχος, -ον: allied, fighting along
    with; (as subst.) ally
ὁ, ἡ, τό: the
οἶδα: to know
οἴομαι: to suppose, think, imagine
ὀλίγος -η, -ον: few, little, small
ὄνομα, -ατος, τό: name
ὁράω: to see, look, behold
ὅς, ἥ, ὅ: who, which, that
ὅτι: that, why; what
οὐ, οὐκ, οὐχ: not
οὗτος, αὕτη, τοῦτο: this, these
πᾶς, πᾶσα, πᾶν: every, all, the whole
πάσχω: to suffer, experience
παύω: to stop, make cease
πείθω: to persuade, win over, trust; mid.
    obey
περί: around, about, concerning
ποιέω: to do, make, create; mid. consider
πόλεμος, ὁ: war, battle, fight
πόλις, -εως, ἡ: a city-state, city
πολύς, πολλά, πολύ: much, many
πράσσω: to do, accomplish, make, act
πρός: to (acc.), near, in addition to (dat.)
πρῶτος, -η, -ον: first, early
σωτηρία, ἡ: deliverance, safety
σώφρων, -ον: prudent, moderate
τε: and, both
τίθημι: to set, put, place, arrange
τις, τι: anyone, -thing; someone, -thing
τίς, τί: who? which?
τρέπω: to turn, direct

τυγχάνω: to chance upon, get; happen
ὑμεῖς: you
φαίνομαι: to appear, seem; to become
    visible, be seen
φέρω: to bear, carry, bring, convey
φημί: to say, claim, assert
φίλος, -η, -ον: friendly; subst. friend, kin
φοβέω: to put to flight, terrify, frighten
φόβος, ὁ: fear, terror, panic
φύσις, -εως, ἡ: nature, character
ὡς: as, thus, so, that; when, since

SYNTAX

Articular infinitive: An article (declinable) with an infinitive; together equivalent to the English gerund (verbal noun)
- τοῦ διδάσκειν: *of instructing* (86)
- ἔξω...τοῦ πλεόνων ἄρξαι: *aside from ruling more (men)* (97)

Article with a participle used as a substantive (noun), often an abstract noun
- τὸ μὴ δοκοῦν: *what does not seem...or that which does not seem..., etc.* (85)
- τὸ εἰκός: *what is likely* (86)
- τὸ ξυμφέρον: *the useful, what is useful* (90)

Article with adjective used as noun, sometimes an abstract noun
- τὸ δίκαιον: *justice, the just, what is just* (90)
- τὸ κοινὸν ἀγαθόν: *the common good, what is commonly recognized as good* (90)
- ἐκ τοῦ θείου: *divine;* lit. *from the divine (i.e. the gods)* (104)

Neuter acc. adjective (sg. or pl.) with or without the article used adverbially
- τὸ πρῶτον: *first, first of all, at first* (84.2)

Impersonal expressions
- (with acc. subj. and inf. verb) εἰκὸς μὲν καὶ ξυγγνώμη ἐν τῷ τοιῷδε καθεστῶτας...τρέπεσθαι: *it is reasonable and a matter worthy of forbearance for those in such a situation to turn* (88)
- (with dative subj. and infin. verb) οἷς παρὸν...σῴζεσθαι: *when it is possible for them to be saved* (103.2)
- εἰ δοκεῖ: *if it seems (good) to you* (with implied ὑμῖν, 88)

Subjective genitive
- τῶν κρατούντων...ἡ λῆψις: *capture by those who rule* (110.1) (τῶν κρατούντων are the ones who capture.)

Objective genitive
- ἡμῶν ἡ ἐς τοὺς ὀλίγους ἀγωγή: *leading us before the few* (85) (ἡμῶν are the ones whom others lead.)

Genitive of comparison with verbs implying difference

- ναυκρατόρων...εἰ μὴ περιγένοισθε: *if you do not prevail over (i.e. are not superior to, or better than) masters of the sea* (97)

The middle of ποιέω + noun equivalent to an active verb

- τὴν παρακινδύνευσιν ποιοῦνται = παρακινδυνεύουσι: *they undertake a great risk* (99)

A future participle used with a verb of motion to express purpose

- λόγους πρῶτον ποιησομένους ἔπεμψαν πρέσβεις: *first they sent envoys to negotiate* (84.3).

Potential optative: ἄν + optative (pres. or aor., where tense expresses aspect, not time) is often used to express potential. Sometimes, but not always, a future condition is implied.

- ξυνελὼν μάλιστ' ἂν δηλώσειεν ὅτι: *in sum he would make very clear that* (105.4)
- παυοίμεθ' ἄν...λέγοιμεν ἄν: *we would stop speaking ...we would continue to speak* (87)

Sometimes an optative may be equivalent to a future. The above example thinly disguises a threat, *we will stop...we will continue to speak* (87)

ἄν with a participle (or infinitive) in indirect statement to represent a potential optative

- εἰδότες καὶ ὑμᾶς ἂν καὶ ἄλλους... δρῶντας ἂν ταὐτό: *knowing that both you and others...would do the same* (105.3)

ABBREVIATIONS

<	from	impf.	imperfect	pl.	plural
abs.	absolute	impers.	impersonal	plpf.	pluperfect
acc.	accusative	indic.	indicative	pot.	potential
act.	active	ind. state.	indirect	pred.	predicate
adj.	adjective		statement	prep.	preposition
adv.	adverb	inf.	infinitive	pres.	present
aor.	aorist	inter.	interrogative	pron.	pronoun
att. circ.	attendant	m.	masculine	rel.	relative
	circumstances	mod	modified	sg.	singular
b/c	because	n.	neuter	subj.	subject
comp.	comparative	nom.	nominative	subj. gen.	subjective
dat.	dative	obj.	object		genitive
demonst.	demonstrative	obj. gen.	objective	subjunct.	subjunctive
dir. obj.	direct object		genitive	superl.	superlative
f.	feminine	opt.	optative	transl.	translate a
fut.	future	ppl.	participle	vs.	as opposed to
gen.	genitive	pass.	passive	w/	with
imper.	imperative	pf.	perfect		

Person and number, when noted, are marked with a number and single letter, denoting singular or plural: 1s, 2s, 3s, 1p, 2p, 3p.

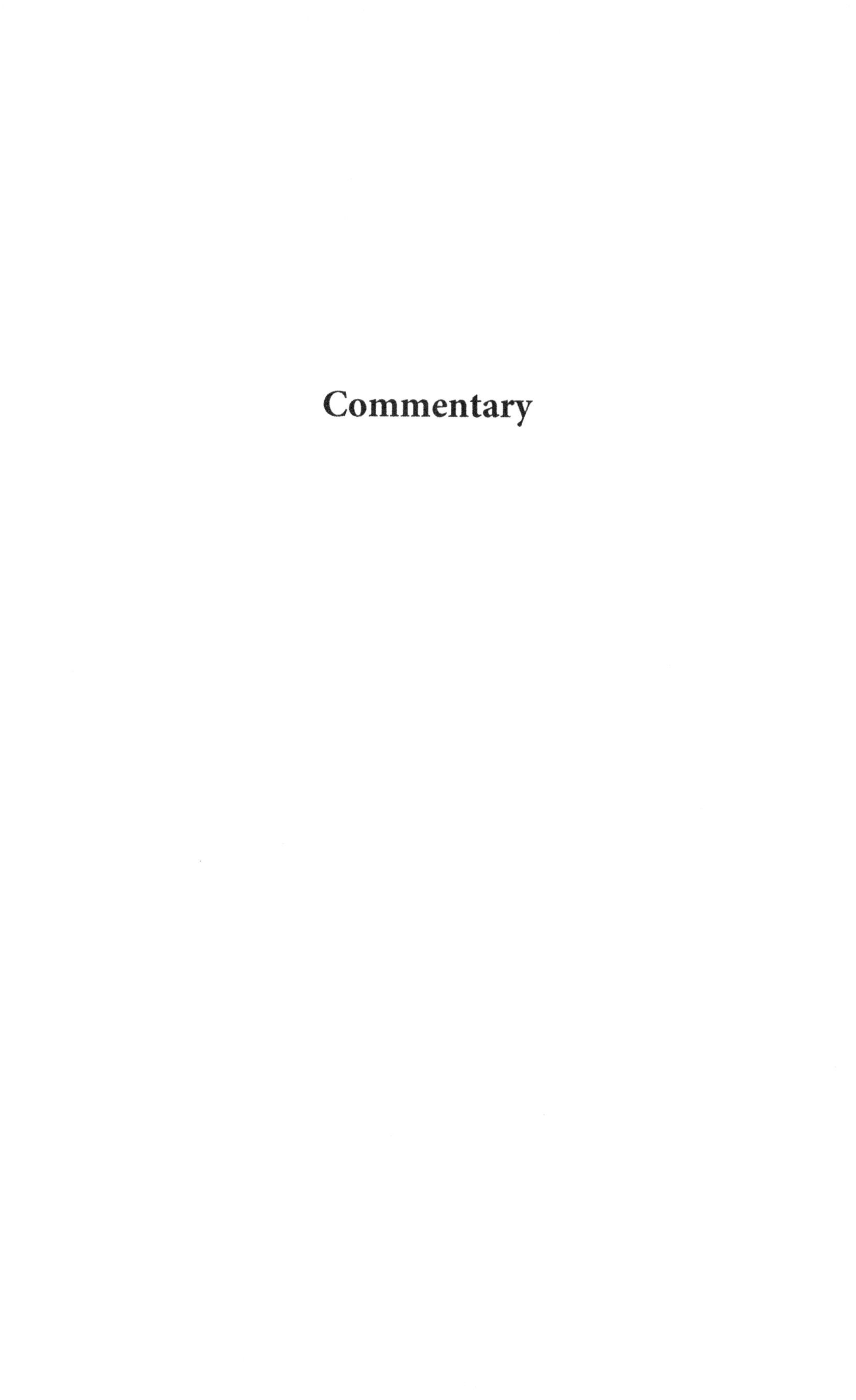

Commentary

Thucydides

Ἀλκιβιάδης, ὁ: Alcibiades, a brilliant Athenian orator (i.e. politician) and commander, related to Pericles. He was opposed to the Peace of 421. Elected in 416 as one of three generals in command of the Sicilian expedition, when called back from Sicily to Athens to stand trial for impiety, he escaped and defected to the Spartans. Later he returned to the Athenians, only to go into self-imposed exile in the Chersonese, where he was killed.

Ἀργεῖος, -α, -ον: Argive, of Argos

Ἄργος, τό: Argos

διακόσιοι, -αι, -α: two hundred

δοκέω: to seem, seem good, think, imagine

ἑαυτοῦ (αὑτοῦ) -ῆς, -οῦ: him-, her-, itself

ἐγγύς: near (gen.); adv. nearby

εἴκοσι: twenty

ἐπι-γίγνομαι: to come after or next, to follow (upon); to befall

θέρος, τό: summer

ἱππο-τοξότης, ὁ: horse-mounted archer

κατα-τίθημι: to put down, deposit, settle

Λέσβιος, -α, -ον: Lesbian, of Lesbos

μάλιστα: most of all; certainly, especially; (with numbers) approximately

Μῆλος, ὁ: Melos

ναῦς, νεώς, ἡ: a ship, boat

νησιῶται, οἱ: islanders

ὁπλίτης, -ου, ὁ: hoplite, armed soldier

πεντακόσιοι, -αι, -α: five hundred

πλέω: to sail

στρατεύω: to march, campaign

τοξότης, ὁ: an archer, bowman

τριάκοντα: thirty

τριακόσιοι, -αι, -α: three hundred

ὕποπτος, -ον: viewed with suspicion

φρονέω: to think, to have (particular kinds of) thoughts; to be wise, prudent; to agree

χίλιοι, -αι, -α: thousand

Χίος, -α, -ον: Chian, of Chios (island)

Τοῦ δ' ἐπιγιγνομένου θέρους Ἀλκιβιάδης τε πλεύσας ἐς 84
Ἄργος ναυσὶν εἴκοσιν Ἀργείων τοὺς δοκοῦντας ἔτι ὑπόπτους
εἶναι καὶ τὰ Λακεδαιμονίων φρονεῖν ἔλαβε τριακοσίους
ἄνδρας, καὶ κατέθεντο αὐτοὺς Ἀθηναῖοι ἐς τὰς ἐγγὺς νήσους
ὧν ἦρχον· καὶ ἐπὶ Μῆλον τὴν νῆσον Ἀθηναῖοι ἐστράτευσαν 25
ναυσὶν ἑαυτῶν μὲν τριάκοντα, Χίαις δὲ ἔξ, Λεσβίαιν δὲ δυοῖν,
καὶ ὁπλίταις ἑαυτῶν μὲν διακοσίοις καὶ χιλίοις καὶ τοξόταις
τριακοσίοις καὶ ἱπποτοξόταις εἴκοσι, τῶν δὲ ξυμμάχων καὶ
νησιωτῶν ὁπλίταις μάλιστα πεντακοσίοις καὶ χιλίοις. οἱ δὲ 2

---

21 **τοῦ...θέρους**: gen. abs. or gen. of time during which
Ἀλκιβιάδης τε...Ἄργος...καὶ ἐπὶ Μῆλον...Ἀθηναῖοι: Thuc. correlates the attacks on Argos and Melos as two big undertakings of the summer of 416 BCE.

22 **τοὺς δοκοῦντας ἔτι**: *the men still seeming*; art. w/ ppl. used as a noun; the other men were executed or in exile.

23 **εἶναι**: inf. w/ δοκοῦντας
τὰ Λακεδαιμονίων φρονεῖν: *to favor the Spartan cause*; inf. w/ δοκοῦντας

24 **κατέθεντο αὐτοὺς Ἀθηναῖοι**: i.e. and put them into custody; κατέθεντο, aor. indic. mid. < κατατίθημι

25 **ὧν**: f. gen. pl. of rel. pron., obj. of ἄρχω
τὴν νῆσον: Melos is also the name of the the city, since it was a one-city island, unlike, e.g., Lesbos.

26 **μὲν...δὲ...δὲ**: i.e. 30 ships of their own (μὲν) plus those of two allies (δὲ...δὲ); both allies were islanders.
Λεσβίαιν: dual dat; most likely they were from the city of Methymna, which had remained an independent tributary ally (unlike Mytilene).

27 **ὁπλίταις...καὶ τοξόταις...καὶ ἱπποτοξόταις**: the three kinds of Athenian land forces
ὁπλίταις ἑαυτῶν μὲν...τῶν δὲ ξυμμάχων: i.e. they used both their own hoplites and hoplites from their allies. Thuc. uses the Ionic ξυ- (ξυμ-, ξυν-) instead of συ- (συμ-, συν-); lexica list definitions under συ- (συμ-, συν-).

28 **καὶ νησιωτῶν**: *(who were) also islanders*. Most likely Thuc. is not distinguishing between allies and unallied islanders.

29 **μάλιστα**: *approximately, about*; a common meaning with numbers

ἀ-δικέω: to be unjust, do wrong, injure

ἀναγκάζω: to force, compel, require

ἄπ-οικος, ὁ: colonist, settler

ἀρχή, ἡ: a beginning; rule, office

δηιόω: to slay, cut down; waste, ravage

ἐθέλω: to be willing, wish, desire

ἔπ-ειτα: then, next, secondly

ἥκω: to have come, be present

ἡσυχάζω: to keep quiet, rest (from war)

καθ-ίστημι: to set up, establish; to

κελεύω: to bid, order, command, exhort

Κλεομήδης, ὁ: Cleomedes; an Athenian general (an elected office) from a
  wealthy family; Thuc. does not mentions Cleomedes elsewhere in the History.

Λυκομήδης, -ους, ὁ: Lycomedes

νησιῶται, οἱ: islanders

οὐδ-έτερος, -η, -ον: neither of the two

οὖν: and so, then; so then; at any event

παρασκευή, ἡ: preparation; intrigue

πλῆθος, τό: crowd, multitude; size

πρέσβυς, -εως, ὁ: old (man), ambassador, envoy

πρίν: until, before

στρατοπεδεύω: to encamp, take a position

στρατός, τό: army, encamped army

Τεισίας, ὁ: Teisias; an Athenian general (an elected office) from a wealthy
  family; Thuc. does not mention Teisias elsewhere in the History.

Τεισίμαχος, ὁ: Teisimachus

ὑπ-ακούω: to heed, listen to (gen.); to yield (to), submit (to), comply (with)
  (dat.)

φανερός, -ά, -όν: visible, manifest, evident

ὥσπερ: as, just as, as if

Μήλιοι Λακεδαιμονίων μέν εἰσιν ἄποικοι, τῶν δ' Ἀθηναίων 1
οὐκ ἤθελον ὑπακούειν ὥσπερ οἱ ἄλλοι νησιῶται, ἀλλὰ τὸ
μὲν πρῶτον οὐδετέρων ὄντες ἡσύχαζον, ἔπειτα ὡς αὐτοὺς
ἠνάγκαζον οἱ Ἀθηναῖοι δῃοῦντες τὴν γῆν, ἐς πόλεμον
φανερὸν κατέστησαν. στρατοπεδευσάμενοι οὖν ἐς τὴν γῆν 3
αὐτῶν τῇ παρασκευῇ ταύτῃ οἱ στρατηγοὶ Κλεομήδης τε ὁ
Λυκομήδους καὶ Τεισίας ὁ Τεισιμάχου, πρὶν ἀδικεῖν τι τῆς
γῆς, λόγους πρῶτον ποιησομένους ἔπεμψαν πρέσβεις. οὓς
οἱ Μήλιοι πρὸς μὲν τὸ πλῆθος οὐκ ἤγαγον, ἐν δὲ ταῖς
ἀρχαῖς καὶ τοῖς ὀλίγοις λέγειν ἐκέλευον περὶ ὧν ἥκουσιν. 10

---

1 **ἄποικοι**: *colonists;* i.e. putatively related by blood and religion, although a broad range of possible ties and obligations could be implied.

3 **οὐδετέρων ὄντες**: i.e. being allies or partisans of neither the Athenians or Spartans
ἡσύχαζον: i.e. they continued to remained neutral.
ὡς: *when*

4 **δῃοῦντες**: contracted pres. ppl. < δῃιόω
ἐς πόλεμον φανερὸν κατέστησαν: *entered into an open state of hostility;* both this and the pillaging seem to refer to the earlier attack in 426. The important point is that they seem not to have participated in the larger conflict between Sp. and Ath., now suspended by the Peace of Nicias (Peace of 421).

5 **οὖν**: The particle marks the return of the narrative to 416.
ἐς τὴν γῆν: ἐς because implicit in the ppl. στρατοπεδουσάμενοι is an initial attack against (ἐς) Melos.

6 **τῇ παρασκευῇ ταύτῃ**: i.e. with those forces mentioned in 5.84.1

7 **πρὶν**: w/ inf. = *before*
τῆς γῆς: partitive gen. w/ τι

8 **λόγους πρῶτον ποιησομένους**: *to confer first;* fut. ppl. w/ verb of motion (πέμπω) to express purpose
οὓς: transl. rel. as demonst.: *these men;* i.e. the envoys

9 **τὸ πλῆθος**: *the multitude;* i.e. "the people," not just the few men in positions of power
ἐν δὲ ταῖς ἀρχαῖς καὶ τοῖς ὀλίγοις: *among the magistrates* (lit. *[men] in offices) and the (privileged) few;* ταῖς ἀρχαῖς should include members of the Council; mention of speaking before the πλῆθος, *the multitude,* points to the existence of an assembly. The official position of "the few," however, is not clear.

10 **περὶ ὧν**: the antecedent of ὧν is the implied object of λέγειν, i.e. the matters to be discussed
ἥκουσιν: *they had come;* the pres. of ἥκω is perfect in sense, so w/ the introductory verb ἐκέλευον transl. ἥκουσιν as a plpf.

ἀγωγή, ἡ: a bringing, a carrying away
ἀλλήλος, -α, -ον: one another
ἀν-έλεγκτος, -ον: not to be questioned
ἀπατάω: to cheat, trick, deceive, beguile
ἀπο-κρίνομαι: to answer, reply
ἀρέσκω: to please, satisfy, appease
ἀ-σφαλής, ές: safe, secure, trusty, not liable to move or fall
δή: indeed, surely, really, certainly, just
διδάσκω: to teach, instruct
δοκέω: to seem, seem good, think, imagine
εἷς, μία, ἕν: one, single, alone
ἕκαστος, -η, -ον: each, every one
ἐπ-αγωγός, -όν: attractive, alluring, luring on
ἐπειδή: when, after, since, because
ἐπι-είκεια, ἡ: reasonableness; equity
ἐπιτήδειος, -η, -ον: suitable; (of provisions) necessary
ἐσ-άπαξ: at once, once of all
εὐθύς: right away, straight, directly, at once
ἡσυχία, ἡ: silence, quiet, stillness, rest
κάθ-ημαι: to sit
κρίνω: to choose, decide; interpret
μηδέ: and not, but not, nor
ξύν-εδρος, ὁ: commissioner, councillor
ξυν-εχής, -ές: continuous
ὅπως: how, in what way; in order that, that
πλῆθος, τό: crowd, multitude; size
πρέσβυς, -εως, ὁ: old, old (man); ambassador, envoy
ῥῆσις, -εως, ἡ: a saying, speech
τοιόσδε, -άδε, -όνδε: such
ὑπο-λαμβάνω: to take up, reply; interrupt; suppose
φρονέω: to think, to have (particular kinds of) thoughts; to be wise, prudent;
    to agree

οἱ δὲ τῶν Ἀθηναίων πρέσβεις ἔλεγον τοιάδε. 'ἐπειδὴ οὐ 85
πρὸς τὸ πλῆθος οἱ λόγοι γίγνονται, ὅπως δὴ μὴ ξυνεχεῖ
ῥήσει οἱ πολλοὶ ἐπαγωγὰ καὶ ἀνέλεγκτα ἐσάπαξ ἀκούσαντες
ἡμῶν ἀπατηθῶσιν (γιγνώσκομεν γὰρ ὅτι τοῦτο φρονεῖ ἡμῶν
ἡ ἐς τοὺς ὀλίγους ἀγωγή), ὑμεῖς οἱ καθήμενοι ἔτι ἀσφαλέ- 15
στερον ποιήσατε. καθ' ἕκαστον γὰρ καὶ μηδ' ὑμεῖς ἑνὶ
λόγῳ, ἀλλὰ πρὸς τὸ μὴ δοκοῦν ἐπιτηδείως λέγεσθαι εὐθὺς
ὑπολαμβάνοντες κρίνετε. καὶ πρῶτον εἰ ἀρέσκει ὡς λέγομεν εἴπατε.'   οἱ δὲ τῶν Μηλίων ξύνεδροι ἀπεκρίναντο 86
'ἡ μὲν ἐπιείκεια τοῦ διδάσκειν καθ' ἡσυχίαν ἀλλήλους 20

---

11 **τοιάδε**: *the following;* it does not, however, imply a verbatim report.

12 **ὅπως δὴ μή**: introduces a neg. purp. clause with δή (*evidently*) giving the actual reason

13 **οἱ πολλοί**: *the many;* i.e. the people vs. τοὺς ὀλίγους, mentioned below
ἀκούσαντες: w/ gen. of person (source) and accus. of what is heard

14 **ἀπατηθῶσιν**: aor. subjunct. pass. < ἀπατάω in neg. purp. clause
τοῦτο φρονεῖ: *means this;* i.e. they infer fear of their persuasive speech from the fact that they have been kept away from the Melian people.
ἡμῶν: obj. gen. w/ ἡ...ἀγωγή, *(your) leading us...*

15 **ἔτι ἀσφαλέστερον**: *even more cautiously;* neut. comp. adj. of ἀσφαλής used as adv.

16 **ποιήσατε**: *proceed* (lit. *do* or *act*); aor. act. imper.

καθ' ἕκαστον: *(respond) point by point* or *concerning each (individual) point*
γάρ: leave untranslated; it introduces what the Athenians mean by acting more cautiously.
καὶ μηδ': *and also not;* i.e. like the Athenians, who will not do this either

17 **τὸ μὴ δοκοῦν**: *whatever does not seem;* art. w/ neut. ppl. (here in acc.) to create a substantive (noun); w/ μή b/c it is generic
λέγεσθαι: inf. w/ δοκοῦν
κρίνετε: *give your judgment;* pres. act. imper.

18 **ὡς λέγομεν**: *our proposal* or *as we propose* (lit. *how we speak*); the clause is the subj. of ἀρέσκει.

19 **εἴπατε**: aor. act. imper.

20 **τοῦ διδάσκειν**: gen. of articular infin.; it limits ἐπιείκεια.
καθ' ἡσυχίαν: *at leisure;* i.e. taking our time, without the distractions of an assembly

βουλεύω: to deliberate, plan, take counsel

δια-φέρω: to carry over; differ, disagree

δουλεία, ἡ: servitude, slavery, bondage

εἰκός, -ότος, τό: likelihood, what is likely, probable, reasonable (neut. pf. ppl. < ἔοικα)

ἐν-δίδωμαι: to give in, surrender; allow

ἥκω: to have come, be present

κριτής, -οῦ, ὁ: judge, decider

λογίζομαι: to reckon, calculate, account

μέλλω: to be about to, intend to

ξυν-ήκω: to have come together, meet

πάρ-ειμι: to be near, be present, be at hand; (impersonal) to be in one's power

περι-γίγνομαι: to prevail over, be superior (to)

σωτηρία, ἡ: deliverance, safety

τελευτή, ἡ: an end, completion, outcome; death

τοί-νυν: well then; therefore, accordingly

ὑπό-νοια, ἡ: suspicion, notion, thought

ψέγω: to blame, censure, find fault with

οὐ ψέγεται, τὰ δὲ τοῦ πολέμου παρόντα ἤδη καὶ οὐ μέλ- 21
λοντα διαφέροντα αὐτοῦ φαίνεται. ὁρῶμεν γὰρ αὐτούς τε
κριτὰς ἥκοντας ὑμᾶς τῶν λεχθησομένων καὶ τὴν τελευτὴν
ἐξ αὐτοῦ κατὰ τὸ εἰκὸς περιγενομένοις μὲν τῷ δικαίῳ καὶ
δι' αὐτὸ μὴ ἐνδοῦσι πόλεμον ἡμῖν φέρουσαν, πεισθεῖσι δὲ 25
δουλείαν.'

ΑΘ. Εἰ μὲν τοίνυν ὑπονοίας τῶν μελλόντων λογιούμενοι 87
ἢ ἄλλο τι ξυνήκετε ἢ ἐκ τῶν παρόντων καὶ ὧν ὁρᾶτε περὶ
σωτηρίας βουλεύσοντες τῇ πόλει, παυοίμεθ' ἄν· εἰ δ' ἐπὶ
τοῦτο, λέγοιμεν ἄν. 30

---

21 **τὰ δὲ τοῦ πολέμου:** *(your) hostile acts* (lit. *things of war*)
παρόντα ἤδη καὶ οὐ μέλλοντα: *before our eyes now and not merely threatened;* modifies τὰ τοῦ πολέμου

22 **διαφέροντα φαίνεται:** *is clearly at odds with it;* i.e. with leisurely instruction; φαίνεται w/ ppl. = *is seen* [to be] vs. w/ inf. = *seems* [to be]
ὁρῶμεν: 'see' intros. two ind. states. w/ accus. subj. and ppl. verb: 1) αὐτούς τε…ὑμᾶς…ἥκοντας and 2) τὴν τελ-ευτὴν …φέρουσαν
αὐτούς τε κρίτας… ὑμᾶς: *yourselves as judges;* κρίτας, masc. acc. pl.

23 **τῶν λεχθησομένων:** *of what will be said;* fut. pass. ppl; w/ art. = noun; it limits κρίτας, *judges of…*
τὴν τελευτὴν: w/ φέρουσαν
ἐξ αὐτοῦ: *(that comes) of it;* i.e. the conference

24 **κατὰ τὸ εἰκὸς:** *in all likelihood*
περιγενομένοις μὲν: *if we win (the debate);* masc. dat. pl. ppl w/ ἡμῖν
τῷ δικαίῳ: *by (the argument of) right,* or *by (our) just (cause)*

25 **δι'αὐτὸ:** *because of it;* i.e. winning
μὴ ἐνδοῦσι: dat. pl. ppl.; expands περιγενομένοις; μὴ b/c conditional

πόλεμον…δουλείαν: objs. of φέρ-ουσαν
πεισθεῖσι δὲ: *if we are persuaded (to give in);* masc. dat. pl. of aor. pass. ppl., also w/ ἡμῖν

27 **τοίνυν:** a conversational particle found only in direct speech in Thuc.
ὑπονοίας τῶν μελλόντων: *surmises concerning the future*
λογιούμενοι: fut. ppl. < λογίζομαι to express purpose

28 **ἄλλο τι…ἢ:** *(intending) anything other than*
ξυνήκετε: *you meet with us* (lit. *you have come together*)
ὧν ὁρᾶτε: parallels τῶν παρόντων; ὧν = ἅ (dir. obj of ὁρᾶτε), which is assimilated into the gen. b/c the whole clause is the second obj. of ἐκ

29 **περὶ σωτηρίας βουλεύσοντες τῇ πόλει:** *to take counsel about the survival of your city (or for your city);* βουλεύσοντες, fut. ppl. to express purpose
παυοίμεθ' ἄν: *we would stop (negotiating);* pres. opt.
ἐπὶ τοῦτο: *for this;* i.e. toward this end, w/ ξυνήκετε
λέγοιμεν ἄν: *…we would continue to speak;* pres. opt.

ἀ-δικέω: to be unjust, do wrong, injure

ἀληθής, -ές: true

ἀξιόω: to deem or think worthy

ἄ-πιστος, -ον: not trustworthy, unreliable; not trusting

ἄπ-οικος, ὁ: colonist, settler

δια-πράσσω: to accomplish, effect

δοκέω: to seem, seem good, think, imagine

δυνατός, -ή, -όν: capable, strong, possible

εἰκός, -ότος, τό: likelihood, what is likely, probable, reasonable (neut. pf. ppl. < ἔοικα)

ἑκάτερος, -α, -ον: each of two, either

ἐπ-εξ-έρχομαι: to go out against; go through; proceed against

καθ-ίστημι: to set up, establish; to become, bring into a certain state

κατα-λύω: to put down, destroy

μέντοι: however, nevertheless; certainly

μετά: with (gen.); after (acc.)

Μῆδος, ὁ: a Mede; the Persians

ξυγ-γνώμη, ἡ: forgiveness, pardon

ξύν-οδος, ἡ: encounter, meeting

ξυ-στρατεύω: to compaign together

ὅδε, ἥδε, τόδε: this

οὐδ-είς, οὐδε-μία, οὐδ-έν: no one, nothing

οὔ-τε: and not, neither...nor

πάρ-ειμι: to be near, be present, be at hand; (impersonal) to be in one's power

παρ-έχω: to provide, furnish, give

προ-καλέω: to call forth; to propose or offer; (mostly mid.) to provoke, challenge

τοί-νυν: well then; therefore, accordingly

τοιόσδε, -άδε, -όνδε: such

τρόπος, ὁ: a manner, way; turn, direction

φρονέω: to think, to have (particular kinds of) thoughts; to be wise, prudent; to agree

ΜΗΛ. Εἰκὸς μὲν καὶ ξυγγνώμη ἐν τῷ τοιῷδε καθεστῶτας 88
ἐπὶ πολλὰ καὶ λέγοντας καὶ δοκοῦντας τρέπεσθαι· ἡ μέντοι
ξύνοδος καὶ περὶ σωτηρίας ἥδε πάρεστι, καὶ ὁ λόγος ᾧ
προκαλεῖσθε τρόπῳ, εἰ δοκεῖ, γιγνέσθω.

ΑΘ. Ἡμεῖς τοίνυν οὔτε αὐτοὶ μετ' ὀνομάτων καλῶν, ὡς ἢ 89
δικαίως τὸν Μῆδον καταλύσαντες ἄρχομεν ἢ ἀδικούμενοι νῦν 6
ἐπεξερχόμεθα, λόγων μῆκος ἄπιστον παρέξομεν, οὔθ' ὑμᾶς
ἀξιοῦμεν ἢ ὅτι Λακεδαιμονίων ἄποικοι ὄντες οὐ ξυνεστρατεύ-
σατε ἢ ὡς ἡμᾶς οὐδὲν ἠδικήκατε λέγοντας οἴεσθαι πείσειν,
τὰ δυνατὰ δ' ἐξ ὧν ἑκάτεροι ἀληθῶς φρονοῦμεν διαπράσ- 10

---

1 **Εἰκὸς μὲν καὶ ξυγγνώμη:** *it is reasonable and pardonable;* infer ἐστὶ; impersonal expression w/ acc. / inf.
ἐν τῷ τοιῷδε: *in such a situation*
καθεστῶτας: *being;* pf. act. ppl. < καθίστημι; acc. subj. of the inf. τρέπεσθαι; understand *men,* not *we.*

2 **καὶ λέγοντας καὶ δοκοῦντας:** *in both speech and thought;* the latter alludes to ὑπονοίας in 5.87.
τρέπεσθαι: *to resort to;* inf. w/ εἰκὸς καὶ ξυγγνώμη
ἡ...ξύνοδος...ἥδε πάρεστι: *this conference at hand is*
μέντοι: *however,* or *be that as it may;* it answers εἰκὸς μὲν, etc.

3 **καὶ περὶ σωτηρίας:** *in fact about survival;* καὶ is emphatic.
ᾧ προκαλεῖσθε τρόπῳ: *as you propose*

4 **εἰ δοκεῖ:** *if you like* (lit. *if it seems good [to you]*)
γιγνέσθω: *let it be (so),* or *let it* [the dialogue] *take place;* pres. mid. imper. 3s; a lukewarm assent at best

5 **οὔτε...παρέξομεν... οὔτε... ἀξιοῦμεν:** despite the grammatical parallel the contrast is between ἡμεῖς αὐτοὶ and ὑμᾶς.

ὀνομάτων καλῶν: i.e. appeals to fine expressions, such as "justice"
ὡς : *that;* intros. ind. state. implied by ὀνομάτων
ἢ...ἢ: intros. what would be the usual justifications; the Aths. dismiss their relevance.

7 **ἐπεξερχόμεθα:** *we proceed against (you);* the verb can connote an attack to seek redress.
λόγων μῆκος ἄπιστον: *a long speech that is not convincing*
οὔθ' ὑμᾶς ἀξιοῦμεν...οἴεσθαι πείσειν: *and you should not suppose that you will convince (us)* (lit. *we deem right that you not suppose,* etc.)

8 **ἢ ὅτι...ἢ ὡς:** ὅτι and ὡς intro. ind. state. w/ λέγοντας; notice that both ind. statements precede the ppl.
οὐ ξυστρατεύσατε: supply αὐτοῖς (the Lacs.)

9 **λέγοντας:** *by saying*

10 **τὰ δύνατα:** dir. obj. of διαπράσ-[σεσθαι]
δ': intros. positive advice vs. earlier negative (οὔτε...οὔθ')
ἐξ ὧν ἑκάτεροι ἀληθῶς φρονοῦμεν: *based on what we each really think*

ἀκριβής, -ές: accurate, precise, exact

ἀνάγκη, ἡ: necessity, force, constraint

ἀνθρώπειος, -α, -ον: human

ἀ-σθενής, -ές: weak, feeble, sick

δή: indeed, surely, really, certainly, just

δυνατός, -ή, -όν: capable, strong, possible

εἰκός, -ότος, τό: likelihood, what is likely, probable, reasonable (neut. pf. ppl. < ἔοικα)

ἐντός: within, inside

ἐπειδή: when, after, since, because

ἐπίσταμαι: to know

ἥσσων, -ον: less, weaker, inferior

κατα-λύω: to put down, destroy

κίνδυνος, ὁ: risk, danger, venture

κρίνω: to choose, decide; interpret

μέγιστος, -η, -ον: greatest, best, longest

ξυγ-χωρέω: to come together, agree, assent

ξυμ-φέρω: to bring together; to come to terms, agree; (of events) to happen; to confer a benefit, be useful, be expedient

οὕτως: in this way, thus, so

παρά: from, from the side of (gen.); beside, alongside (dat.); to the side of; past, beyond; compared to (acc.)

παρά-δειγμα, τό: example, proof

προ-έχω: to hold forth; be first, surpass, excel

σφάλλω: to make fall, overthrow, defeat; frustrate; (pass.) be overthrown; go wrong, be frustrated, be mistaken in something (gen.)

τιμωρία, ἡ: punishment; help, aid

ὑπο-τίθημι: to place under, advise, propose

χρήσιμος, -η, -ον: good, useful, serviceable

ὠφελέω: to benefit, help; be profitable

σεσθαι, ἐπισταμένους πρὸς εἰδότας ὅτι δίκαια μὲν ἐν τῷ   11
ἀνθρωπείῳ λόγῳ ἀπὸ τῆς ἴσης ἀνάγκης κρίνεται, δυνατὰ δὲ
οἱ προύχοντες πράσσουσι καὶ οἱ ἀσθενεῖς ξυγχωροῦσιν.

MHΛ. Ἦι μὲν δὴ νομίζομέν γε, χρήσιμον (ἀνάγκη γάρ,   90
ἐπειδὴ ὑμεῖς οὕτω παρὰ τὸ δίκαιον τὸ ξυμφέρον λέγειν   15
ὑπέθεσθε) μὴ καταλύειν ὑμᾶς τὸ κοινὸν ἀγαθόν, ἀλλὰ τῷ
αἰεὶ ἐν κινδύνῳ γιγνομένῳ εἶναι τὰ εἰκότα καὶ δίκαια, καί τι
καὶ ἐντὸς τοῦ ἀκριβοῦς πείσαντά τινα ὠφεληθῆναι. καὶ
πρὸς ὑμῶν οὐχ ἧσσον τοῦτο, ὅσῳ καὶ ἐπὶ μεγίστῃ τιμωρίᾳ
σφαλέντες ἂν τοῖς ἄλλοις παράδειγμα γένοισθε.   20

---

11 [διαπράσ]σεσθαι: *(we should) try obtain;* supply ἀξιοῦμεν; this inf. parallels οἴεσθαι πείσειν, but "we" now mean both sides. Note: Thuc. uses the Ionic σσ not the Attic ττ.
ἐπισταμένους πρὸς εἰδότας: *since we both know* (lit. *men who know before men who know*); it does not matter which ppl. refers to whom.
δίκαια μὲν: n. nom. pl. w/ sg. verb
τῷ ἀνθρωπείῳ λόγῳ: *by human estimation;* i.e. reasoning in a practical way about the human world

12 ἀπὸ: *from the standpoint of*
δυνατὰ: *what they can;* dir. obj. of πράσσουσι, *do* or *exact,* as of a payment or punishment. The contrasts here are both strong vs. weak and action vs. acquiescence.
οἱ προύχοντες: *the stronger;* i.e. men superior in force (ἀνάγκη)

14 Ἦι μὲν δὴ νομίζομέν γε: *as we indeed, at least, believe*
χρήσιμον: supply ἐστι; impersonal expression on which μὴ καταλύειν, εἶναι, and ὠφεληθῆναι all depend
ἀνάγκη: *we must (do this);* i.e. speak of advantage

15 παρὰ τὸ δίκαιον: *(setting) aside (the question of) what is just*

λέγειν ὑπέθεσθε: *you established (as a principle) to speak of...;* ὑπέθεσθε aor. mid. < ὑποτίθημι

16 μὴ καταλύειν: w/ χρήσιμον [ἐστι].
ἀλλὰ τῷ αἰεί ἐν κινδύνῳ γιγνομένῳ: *but for one who is at any time in danger*

17 εἶναι τὰ εἰκότα καὶ δίκαια: *(that) what is reasonable is also just;* w/ χρήσιμον [ἐστί]; alternatively *what is reasonable and just (is useful)*
καί τι καί ἐντὸς τοῦ ἀκριβοῦς πείσαντα τινα ὠφεληθῆναι: *and that, if someone makes a case, even short of the strict limit, he benefit;* ὠφεληθῆναι aor. pass. inf. < ὠφελέω; the third inf. subj. of χρήσιμον [ἐστί]

19 πρὸς ὑμῶν οὐχ ἧσσον: *more for your benefit;* "not less = more" is a rhetorical figure called *litotes;* here the Mels. tactfully cast a warning as what is more beneficial for the Aths.
ὅσῳ καὶ ἐπὶ μεγίστῃ τιμωρίᾳ... γένοισθε: *inasmuch as (you), (being) subject to the greatest vengeance,... would also be*

20 σφαλέντες: *were you to fall;* i.e. to be defeated; aor. pass. ppl. as cond. (fut. less vivid)

ἀγών, ὁ: contest, trial
ἀ-θυμέω: to be disheartened, lose hope for; fear greatly
ἀμφότερος, -α, -ον: each of two, both
ἄ-πονος, -ον: without toil, untroubled
ἀρχή, ἡ: a beginning; rule, office
ἀφ-ίημι: to send forth, let go free; give up
δηλόω: to make clear, show, reveal
ἐπι-τίθημι: to put upon; add; set upon, attack
ἐρέω: will speak (fut. of λέγω)
ἡμέτερος, -α, -ον: our, ours
ἤν (ἐάν, εἰ ἂν): if, if ever
κινδινεύω: to risk, venture; to be probable
κρατέω: to be strong; conquer, prevail
νικάω: to conquer, defeat, win
πάρ-ειμι: to be near, be present, be at hand; (impersonal) to be in one's
    power
που: anywhere, somewhere; I suppose
σῴζω: to save, keep, preserve
σωτηρία, ἡ: deliverance, safety
τελευτή, ἡ: an end, completion, outcome; death
ὑμέτερος, -α, -ον: your, yours
ὑπ-ήκοος, ον: heeding, obeying; being subject to
χρήσιμος, -η, -ον: good, useful, serviceable
ὥσπερ: as, just as, as if
ὠφελία, ἡ: benefit, help

ΑΘ. Ἡμεῖς δὲ τῆς ἡμετέρας ἀρχῆς, ἢν καὶ παυθῇ, οὐκ 91
ἀθυμοῦμεν τὴν τελευτήν· οὐ γὰρ οἱ ἄρχοντες ἄλλων, ὥσπερ
καὶ Λακεδαιμόνιοι, οὗτοι δεινοὶ τοῖς νικηθεῖσιν (ἔστι δὲ οὐ
πρὸς Λακεδαιμονίους ἡμῖν ὁ ἀγών), ἀλλ' ἢν οἱ ὑπήκοοί που
τῶν ἀρξάντων αὐτοὶ ἐπιθέμενοι κρατήσωσιν. καὶ περὶ μὲν 2
τούτου ἡμῖν ἀφείσθω κινδυνεύεσθαι· ὡς δὲ ἐπ' ὠφελίᾳ τε 26
πάρεσμεν τῆς ἡμετέρας ἀρχῆς καὶ ἐπὶ σωτηρίᾳ νῦν τοὺς
λόγους ἐροῦμεν τῆς ὑμετέρας πόλεως, ταῦτα δηλώσομεν,
βουλόμενοι ἀπόνως μὲν ὑμῶν ἄρξαι, χρησίμως δ' ὑμᾶς
ἀμφοτέροις σωθῆναι. 30

---

21 **Ἡμεῖς δὲ:** <u>we</u>, *though*; i.e. the ones
concerned
ἀρχῆς: limiting τελευτήν
ἢν καὶ παυθῇ: *if, in fact, it is (ever)
checked*; παυθῇ, aor. pass. subjunct.

22 **τὴν τελευτήν:** dir. obj. of οὐκ
ἀθυμοῦμεν
ὥσπερ καὶ Λακεδαιμόνιοι: *even as
(is true of) the Lacs.*

23 **οὗτοι:** refers back to and emphasizes
οἱ ἄρχοντες ἄλλων
τοῖς νικηθεῖσιν: *toward the vanquished*; aor. pass. ppl.

24 **ἡμῖν ὁ ἀγών:** *the struggle for us*
**ἢν οἱ ὑπήκοοί που τῶν ἀρξάντων
αὐτοὶ ἐπιθέμενοι κρατήσωσιν:** *if
men who are anywhere subject to
rulers themselves attack (their rulers)
and prevail*; ἐπιθέμενοι, aor. mid. ppl.
< ἐπιτίθημι; κρατήσωσιν, aor.
subjunct. w/ ἢν in a gen. condition,
although the Aths. clearly allude to
their own situation. The cond. explains the real contest and the men
who are truly dangeous (δεινοί).

26 **τούτου:** *this*; i.e. the hostility of allies
ἡμῖν ἀφείσθω κινδυνεύεσθαι:
leave the risk to us or more literally, *let

the risk be left to us; ἀφείσθω, aor.
pass. imper. 3s with inf. κινδυνεύεσθαι as subj.
ὡς: *that* or *how*
ἐπ' ὠφελίᾳ... καὶ ἐπὶ σωτηρίᾳ: ἐπὶ
w/ dat. to express purpose

27 **τοὺς λόγους:** *proposals* or *conditions*

28 **ταῦτα δηλώσομεν:** the pron. refers
back to the preceding ὡς clause expressing their two purposes in speaking.

29 **βουλόμενοι:** *since we wish* or *with
the wish*; understand the ppl. w/ both
ἄρξαι and σωθῆναι.
ἄρξαι: aor. act. inf.; supply *we* as
subj.; ὑμῶν is the gen. obj. of the inf.
ἀπόνως μὲν: *without trouble*; i.e. *for
us*; i.e. without having to lay siege to
the island
χρησίμως δ'...ἀμφοτέροις: *to the
advantage of both (of us)*

30 **σωθῆναι:** aor. pass. inf. < σῴζω, w/
acc. subj. ὑμᾶς

ἀντί: in place of; for the sake of (gen.)

ἀ-σθένεια, ἡ: weakness, feebleness

βλάπτω: to harm, hurt, damage

δηλόω: to make clear, show, reveal

δια-φθείρω: to destroy utterly, disable

δουλεύω: to be a slave, serve, be subject to

δύναμις, -εως, ἡ: power, force, capacity

ἔχθρα, ἡ: hatred

ἡσυχία, ἡ: silence, quiet, stillness, rest

κερδαίνω: to gain, make a profit

μηδ-έτερος, -η, -ον: neither of the two

μῖσος, -εος, τό: hate, hatred

ξυμ-βαίνω: to stand with; come to an agreement; to happen, turn out (in a
    certain way)

παρά-δειγμα, τό: example, proof

πολέμιος, -α, -ον: hostile, of the enemy

πρό: before, in front; in place of (gen.)

πῶς: how? in what way?

τοσοῦτος, -αύτη, -οῦτο: so (or such) great, so many, so much

ὑπ-ακούω: to heed, listen to (gen.); to yield, submit, comply (dat.)

φιλία, ἡ: friendship, affection, love

χρήσιμος, -η, -ον: good, useful, serviceable

ὥσπερ: as, just as, as if

ὥστε: so that, that, so as to, and so

ΜΗΛ. Καὶ πῶς χρήσιμον ἂν ξυμβαίη ἡμῖν δουλεῦσαι, 92
ὥσπερ καὶ ὑμῖν ἄρξαι;

ΑΘ. Ὅτι ὑμῖν μὲν πρὸ τοῦ τὰ δεινότατα παθεῖν ὑπα- 93
κοῦσαι ἂν γένοιτο, ἡμεῖς δὲ μὴ διαφθείραντες ὑμᾶς κερδαί-
νοιμεν ἄν.   5

ΜΗΛ. Ὥστε [δὲ] ἡσυχίαν ἄγοντας ἡμᾶς φίλους μὲν 94
εἶναι ἀντὶ πολεμίων, ξυμμάχους δὲ μηδετέρων, οὐκ ἂν
δέξαισθε;

ΑΘ. Οὐ γὰρ τοσοῦτον ἡμᾶς βλάπτει ἡ ἔχθρα ὑμῶν ὅσον 95
ἡ φιλία μὲν ἀσθενείας, τὸ δὲ μῖσος δυνάμεως παράδειγμα   10
τοῖς ἀρχομένοις δηλούμενον.

---

1 **χρήσιμον**: n. sg. nom., pred. adj.
modifying aor. inf. δουλεῦσαι, the
subj. of ξυμβαίη
ἂν ξυμβαίη: *could (being slaves)
possibly turn out (to be)*; aor. opt. <
ξυμβαίνω w/ ἄν to express potential
ἡμῖν: dat. w/ χρήσιμον

2 **ὥσπερ καὶ**: *as (it is)*
ὑμῖν ἄρξαι: *for you to rule*; supply
χρήσιμον ἐστί.

3 **πρὸ τοῦ...παθεῖν**: *instead of suffering*;
πρό w/ gen. of art. infin. as obj.
ὑπακοῦσαι: *to submit*; aor. inf., subj.
of γένοιτο. The Aths. use a milder term
than the Mels.' δουλεῦσαι.

4 **ἂν γένοιτο**: *would be*; supply χρήσιμον.
μὴ διαφθείραντες: *were we not to
destroy*; μή indicates the ppl. is cond.
κερδαίνομεν ἄν: opt. w/ ἄν in
apodosis of a fut. less vivid cond.

6 **Ὥστε...ἡμᾶς...οὐκ ἂν δέξαισθε**:
and so you would not allow us...; lit.
accept (that)
[δέ]: δέ should be ignored. Absent
from most manuscripts, it may have

been inserted due to a misunder-
standing of ὥστε.
ἡσυχίαν ἄγοντας: *remaining quiet*;
i.e. by remaining neutral; the ppl.
modifies ἡμᾶς.
φίλους μὲν εἶναι ἀντὶ πολεμίων:
to be friends rather than enemies;
φίλους modifies ἡμᾶς; accus. / inf.
w/ δέξαισθε (*allow*). The Mels.
quickly explain· friends but not allies.

7 **ξυμμάχους δὲ μηδετέρων**: i.e. of
neither the Athenians or Spartans;
supply εἶναι.

9 **Οὐ γὰρ**: *No, for...*; i.e. *We would
not allow you to do this, for...*
ἡ ἔχθρα ὑμῶν: *your hatred (of us)*

10 **ἀσθενείας**: gen. w/ παράδειγμα
δυνάμεως: gen. w/ παράδειγμα
μὲν...δὲ: there are two contrasts, ἡ
φιλία vs. τὸ μῖσος and ἀσθενείας vs.
δυνάμεως.
παράδειγμα...δηλούμενον: *(is)
clearly proof* or *is clear proof*; παρά-
δειγμα, pred. noun w/ both ἡ φιλία
and τὸ μῖσος

ἄλλως: otherwise, in another way; in vain

ἄπ-οικος, ὁ: colonist, settler

ἀ-σθενής, -ές: weak, feeble, sick

ἀ-σφαλής, -ές: safe, secure, trusty, not liable to move or fall

ἀφ-ίστημι: to revolt; withdraw, stand afar

δικαίωμα, τό: plea of right, justification, act setting a wrong right

δύναμις, -εως, ἡ: power, force, capacity

εἰκός, -ότος, τό: likelihood, what is likely, probable, reasonable (neut. pf. ppl. < ἔοικα)

ἐλλείπω: to fall short, lack; leave behind

ἔξω: out of, aside from (gen.)

ἐπ-έρχομαι: to come upon; attack

ἕτερος, -α, -ον: one of two, other, different

ἡγέομαι: to lead; consider, think, believe

κατα-στρέφω: to upset, overturn; (mid.) subdue

ναυ-κράτωρ, ὁ: master of the sea, (lit.) master of a ship

νησιῶται, οἱ: islanders

οὐδ-έτερος, -η, -ον: neither of the two

οὕτως: in this way, thus, so

παρ-έχω: to provide, furnish, give

περι-γίγνομαι: to prevail over, be superior (to)

πλέων, -ον: more, greater

προσ-ήκω: to have come, be present; to be fitting or proper; to belong to, concern

σκοπέω: to look at, examine, consider

ὑπ-ήκοος, -ον: heeding, obeying, be subject to

χειρόω: to subdue, master

ὥστε: so that, that, so as to, and so

ΜΗΛ. Σκοποῦσι δ' ὑμῶν οὕτως οἱ ὑπήκοοι τὸ εἰκός, 96 ὥστε τούς τε μὴ προσήκοντας καὶ ὅσοι ἄποικοι ὄντες οἱ πολλοὶ καὶ ἀποστάντες τινὲς κεχείρωνται ἐς τὸ αὐτὸ τιθέασιν; 15

ΑΘ. Δικαιώματι γὰρ οὐδετέρους ἐλλείπειν ἡγοῦνται, 97 κατὰ δύναμιν δὲ τοὺς μὲν περιγίγνεσθαι, ἡμᾶς δὲ φόβῳ οὐκ ἐπιέναι· ὥστε ἔξω καὶ τοῦ πλεόνων ἄρξαι καὶ τὸ ἀσφαλὲς ἡμῖν διὰ τὸ καταστραφῆναι ἂν παράσχοιτε, ἄλλως τε καὶ νησιῶται ναυκρατόρων καὶ ἀσθενέστεροι ἑτέρων ὄντες εἰ μὴ 20 περιγένοισθε.

---

12 **οὕτως:** explained by ὥστε clause
τὸ εἰκός: *fairness* or *reasonableness*; dir. obj. of σκοποῦσι

13 **ὥστε...τιθέασιν:** *that they place* or *count as;* ὥστε w/ finite verb in actual (vs. natural) result
τούς τε μὴ προσήκοντας: *men with no connection (with you)*; dir. obj. of τιθέασιν
ὅσοι...κεχείρωνται: *those who* (lit. *however many)...have been subdued;* the clause is dir. obj. of τιθέασιν; κεχείρωνται, pf. pass. < χειρόω
ἄποικοι ὄντες οἱ πολλοὶ καὶ ἀποστάντες τινὲς: *many being colonists, some even having rebelled*

14 **ἐς τὸ αὐτὸ:** *in the same category* or *as the same* (depending on the translation of τιθέασιν)

16 **Δικαιώματι γὰρ...:** *(Yes, they do), for by a measure of justice...*
οὐδετέρους ἐλλείπειν: *(that) neither falls short;* i.e. neither allies nor men with no relation to Athens; acc. / inf. in ind. state. w/ ἡγοῦνται

17 **κατὰ δύναμιν δὲ:** *but (they think that it is) a matter of power* (lit. *in accordance with power)*
τοὺς μὲν περιγίγνεσθαι: *that some*

prevail; i.e. remain independent; acc. / inf. in ind. state. w/ ἡγοῦνται
ἡμᾶς δὲ...οὐκ ἐπιέναι: *while we do not attack (them)*; acc. / inf. in ind. state; contrasted w/ τοὺς μὲν περιγίγνεσθαι

18 **ἔξω καὶ:** *even leaving aside*
τοῦ πλεόνων ἄρξαι: gen. art. infin., obj. of prep. ἔξω, while πλεόνων is gen. obj. of ἄρξαι
τὸ ἀσφαλὲς: *security*; dir. obj. of ἂν παράσχοιτε

19 **διὰ τὸ καταστραφῆναι:** *through (your) being subdued;* aor. pass. art. inf., obj. of διά
ἂν παράσχοιτε: aor. opt. < παρέχω. The English construction is: *your conquest would provide (security)*
ἄλλως τε καὶ: *especially*

20 **νησιῶται:** w/ ppl. ὄντες
ναυκρατόρων: *masters of the sea* (lit. *of ships*); gen. obj. of περιγένοισθε; juxtaposing νησιῶται and ναυκρατόρων disrupts the word order.
καὶ ἀσθενέστεροι ἑτέρων ὄντες: *and being weaker than other islanders*
εἰ μὴ περιγένοισθε: *were you not to prevail over;* aor. opt. mid. < περιγίγνομαι; w/ gen.

ἄκων (ἀ-έκων), ἄκουσα, ἄκον: unwilling

ἀ-σφάλεια, ἡ: security, assurance

αὖ: again, once more; further, moreover

βλέπω: to look at, see

δεῖ: it is necessary; one must, ought (+ inf.)

διδάσκω: to teach, instruct

ἐκ-βιβάζω: to make go out, cause to go out; to stop one from

ἐκεῖνος, -η, -ον: that, those

ἐνταῦθα: here, hither, there, thither, then

ἐπ-άγω: to bring to or against; urge

ἡγέομαι: to lead; consider, think, believe

ἥκω: to have come, be present

μεγαλύνω: to make great, strengthen, exalt

μέλλω: to be about to, intend to

μηδέ: and not, but not, nor

μηδ-έτερος, -η, -ον: neither of the two

ξυμ-βαίνω: to stand with; come to an agreement; to happen, turn out (in a certain way)

ξυμ-μαχέω: to fight along side, be an ally

ξύμ-φορος, -ον: advantageous, useful, expedient; (as subst.) interest, advantage

ὅδε, ἥδε, τόδε: this

ὅταν: ὅτε ἄν, whenever

πειράω: to attempt, endeavor, try

πολέμιος, -α, -ον: hostile, of the enemy

πολεμόω: to make hostile, make an enemy (also in mid.)

πῶς: how? in what way?

σφεῖς: they

ὑμέτερος, -α, -ον: your, yours

ὑπ-ακούω: to heed, listen to (gen.); to yield (to), submit (to), comply (with) (dat.)

ὑπ-άρχω: to be there, exist, be ready, be available

χρήσιμος, -η, -ον: good, useful, serviceable

ὥσπερ: as, just as, as if

ΜΗΛ. Ἐν δ' ἐκείνῳ οὐ νομίζετε ἀσφάλειαν; δεῖ γὰρ αὖ 98
καὶ ἐνταῦθα, ὥσπερ ὑμεῖς τῶν δικαίων λόγων ἡμᾶς ἐκβιβάσαντες τῷ ὑμετέρῳ ξυμφόρῳ ὑπακούειν πείθετε, καὶ ἡμᾶς
τὸ ἡμῖν χρήσιμον διδάσκοντας, εἰ τυγχάνει καὶ ὑμῖν τὸ 25
αὐτὸ ξυμβαῖνον, πειρᾶσθαι πείθειν. ὅσοι γὰρ νῦν μηδε-
τέροις ξυμμαχοῦσι, πῶς οὐ πολεμώσεσθε αὐτούς, ὅταν ἐς
τάδε βλέψαντες ἡγήσωνταί ποτε ὑμᾶς καὶ ἐπὶ σφᾶς ἥξειν;
κἂν τούτῳ τί ἄλλο ἢ τοὺς μὲν ὑπάρχοντας πολεμίους
μεγαλύνετε, τοὺς δὲ μηδὲ μελλήσαντας γενέσθαι ἄκοντας 30
ἐπάγεσθε;

---

21 **ἐκείνῳ**: *in that;* i.e. in our offer (of neutrality)
αὖ καὶ ἐνταῦθα: *again even here*

22 **τῶν δικαίων λόγων**: *words* [or *arguments*] *about what is just*
ἡμᾶς ἐκβιβάσαντες: *since you diverted us* or *have kept us from;* aor. ppl. < ἐκβιβάζω; w/ gen. λόγων
24 **τῷ ὑμετέρῳ ξυμφόρῳ ὑπακούειν**: *to comply with (considerations of) your advantage,* inf. w/ ἡμᾶς…πείθετε; i.e. the Mels. are to privilege the interests of the Aths.
πείθετε: *you prevail upon us*
καὶ ἡμᾶς: *(that) we, too;* acc. subj. of inf. πειρᾶσθαι, w/ δεῖ

25 **διδάσκοντας**: *by offering instruction in;* w/ acc. of thing taught; the ppl. modifies ἡμᾶς.
εἰ τυγχάνει…τὸ αὐτὸ ξυμβαῖνον: *if the same thing turns out to be (useful);* τυγχάνει w/ ppl. ξυνβαῖνον = ξυμβαίνει
καὶ ὑμῖν: *to you, too*

26 **πείθειν**: w/ inf. w/ πειρᾶσθαι

27 **ἐς τάδε**: *at this;* i.e. at what the Aths. are doing to Melos

28 **ἡγήσωνταί**: *they consider* or *believe;* aor. subjunct. in fut. more vivid cond. w/ temporal cond. clause (ὅταν in l. 27)
ποτε ὑμᾶς καὶ ἐπὶ σφᾶς ἥξειν: *that at some point you will also attack them;* acc. / inf. in ind. state. w/ ἡγήσωνται

29 **κἂν τούτῳ**: *and therein;* i.e. in acting in this way, or in creating this suspicion; κἂν = καὶ ἐν
τί ἄλλο ἢ: *what else (do you do) than*

30 **μεγαλύνετε**: *increase the number of;* in English the "you" of the verb is expressed in "what else (do you do) than."
τοὺς δὲ μηδὲ μελλήσαντας: *who had no (previous) intention,* or *who did not (otherwise) intend*
γενέσθαι: supply πολεμίους
ἄκοντας: *against their will;* i.e. although they would rather not

31 **ἐπάγεσθε**: *urge* or *induce* (See above note on μεγαλύνετε.)

ἀ-λόγιστος, -ον: unreasonable, thoughtless; reckless, rash

ἀναγκαῖος, -α, -ον: necessary, inevitable

ἄν-αρκτος, -ον: not governed, ungoverned

ἀπ-αλλάσσω: to set free, release from; to end, leave off, cease from; (mid.) to depart

ἄρα: then, therefore, it seems, it turns out

ἀρχή, ἡ: a beginning; rule, office

δειλία, ἡ: cowardice

δια-μέλλησις, -εως, ἡ: postponement, intention

δουλεύω: to be a slave, serve, be subject to

ἐλεύθερος, -η, -ον: free

ἐπ-εξ-έρχομαι: to go out against, proceed against; go through

ἐπι-τρέπω: to turn toward; turn over to, entrust to; rely on

ἦ: truly, in truth

ἠπειρώτης, ὁ: mainlander

καθ-ίστημι: to set up, establish; to become, bring into a certain state

κακότης, ητος, ἡ: baseness, cowardice

κίνδυνος, ὁ: risk, danger, venture

νησιῶται, οἱ: islanders

παρα-κινδύνευσις, -εως, ἡ: a desperate venture

παρ-οξύνω: to urge on, provoke; irritate

πλεῖστος, -η, -ον: most, very many

που: anywhere, somewhere; I suppose

πρό: before, in front; in place of (gen.)

πρό-οπτος, -ον: foreseen, manifest

σφεῖς: they

τοσοῦτος, -αύτη, -οῦτο: so (or such) great, so many, so much

φυλακή, ἡ: guard, a watch, garrison

ὥσπερ: as, just as, as if

ΑΘ. Οὐ γὰρ νομίζομεν ἡμῖν τούτους δεινοτέρους ὅσοι 99
ἠπειρῶταί που ὄντες τῷ ἐλευθέρῳ πολλὴν τὴν διαμέλλησιν
τῆς πρὸς ἡμᾶς φυλακῆς ποιήσονται, ἀλλὰ τοὺς νησιώτας τέ
που ἀνάρκτους, ὥσπερ ὑμᾶς, καὶ τοὺς ἤδη τῆς ἀρχῆς τῷ
ἀναγκαίῳ παροξυνομένους. οὗτοι γὰρ πλεῖστ' ἂν τῷ ἀλο- 5
γίστῳ ἐπιτρέψαντες σφᾶς τε αὐτοὺς καὶ ἡμᾶς ἐς πρόῦπτον
κίνδυνον καταστήσειαν.

ΜΗΛ. Ἦ που ἄρα, εἰ τοσαύτην γε ὑμεῖς τε μὴ παυθῆναι 100
ἀρχῆς καὶ οἱ δουλεύοντες ἤδη ἀπαλλαγῆναι τὴν παρακινδύνευσιν ποιοῦνται, ἡμῖν γε τοῖς ἔτι ἐλευθέροις πολλὴ κακότης 10
καὶ δειλία μὴ πᾶν πρὸ τοῦ δουλεῦσαι ἐπεξελθεῖν.

---

1 **Οὐ γὰρ νομίζομεν…:** *(We disagree),
for we do not think…*
τούτους: explained by ὅσοι…
δεινοτέρους: *more dangerous*
2 **που:** *anywhere;* i.e. wherever they are
τῷ ἐλευθέρῳ: *because of their (sense
of) freedom (from threat)* or *in their
freedom…* (dat. of attend. circ.)
τὴν διαμέλλησιν…ποιήσονται: =
διαμελλήσουσι: *postpone*
3 **τῆς…φυλακῆς:** *(taking) precaution;*
obj. gen. w/ διαμέλλησιν
τοὺς νησιώτας τέ που ἀνάρκτους:
islanders anywhere not ruled (by us);
the art. τοὺς designates a class; supply
νομίζομεν δεινοτέρους w/ this and
τοὺς…παροξυνομένους (below).
καὶ τοὺς ἤδη…παροξυνομένους:
and those already provoked
τῆς ἀρχῆς τῷ ἀναγκαίῳ: *by the
compelling force of our rule*
5 **πλεῖστα…τῷ ἀλογίστῳ ἐπιτρέψαντες:** *by entrusting most (everything)
to recklessness* (lit. *the unreasonable*)
ἂν…καταστήσειαν: *would set,* or
would put; aor. opt. < καθίστημι

6 **ἐς πρόῦπτον κίνδυνον:** *into manifest danger;* i.e. clear and present
danger
8 **Ἦ που ἄρα:** *surely then, we suppose;*
After this sarcastic turning point the
Mels. are increasingly defiant; they
take the lead and speak at greater
length, as do the Aths. in reply.
τοσαύτην γε: supply παρακινδύνευσιν ποιεῖσθε; the particle γε (as in
l. 10) is emphatic.
ὑμεῖς: the nom. pron. is emphatic.
μὴ παυθῆναι…ἀπαλλαγῆναι: *so as
not to cease from…so as to be free of;*
aor. pass. infs. to express purpose;
both w/ gen.
9 **τὴν παρακινδύνευσιν ποιοῦνται:**
*they undertake such a desperate
venture;* w/ τοσαύτην (l. 8); the prefix
παρα- connotes excess.
10 **πολλὴ κακότης καὶ δειλία:** *it is
great baseness and cowardice;*
explained by the following infin.
11 **μὴ πᾶν…ἐπεξελθεῖν:** *not to do and
suffer* (lit. *go through*) *everything*
πρὸ τοῦ δουλεῦσαι: *before becom-
ing slaves* or *rather than become slaves*

ἀγών, ὁ: contest, trial

αἰσχύνη, ἡ: shame, disgrace, dishonor

ἀνδρ-αγαθία, ἡ: bravery, manly virtue

ἀν-έλπιστος, -ον: hopeless, having no hope

ἀνθ-ίστημι: to set against; stand against

βουλεύω: to deliberate, plan, take counsel

βουλή, ἡ: council, plan, will

δια-φέρω: to carry over; differ, disagree

δράω: to do, act

εἴκω: to yield, give way, retire

ἑκάτερος, -α, -ον: each of two, either

εὐθύς: right away, straight, directly, at once

ἐπίσταμαι: to know

κρείσσων, -ον: better, stronger, superior

μᾶλλον: more, rather

μετά: with (gen.); after (acc.)

ὀρθῶς: correctly, straightly, rightly

ὀφλισκάνω (aor. ὦφλον): to owe; be liable to pay a fine; be found guilty; to incur a charge of, bring upon oneself (acc.)

πλῆθος, τό: crowd, multitude; size

ΑΘ.   Οὔκ, ἤν γε σωφρόνως βουλεύησθε· οὐ γὰρ περὶ 101
ἀνδραγαθίας ὁ ἀγὼν ἀπὸ τοῦ ἴσου ὑμῖν, μὴ αἰσχύνην ὀφλεῖν,
περὶ δὲ σωτηρίας μᾶλλον ἡ βουλή, πρὸς τοὺς κρείσσονας
πολλῷ μὴ ἀνθίστασθαι.   15

ΜΗΛ.   Ἀλλ' ἐπιστάμεθα τὰ τῶν πολέμων ἔστιν ὅτε 102
κοινοτέρας τὰς τύχας λαμβάνοντα ἢ κατὰ τὸ διαφέρον
ἑκατέρων πλῆθος· καὶ ἡμῖν τὸ μὲν εἶξαι εὐθὺς ἀνέλπιστον,
μετὰ δὲ τοῦ δρωμένου ἔτι καὶ στῆναι ἐλπὶς ὀρθῶς.   19

---

12 **Οὔκ:** *No;* i.e. *No, it will not be
depravity and cowardice*
ἤν γε…βουλεύησθε: pres.
subjunct. mid. in implied fut. more
vivid cond; γε, *at least*

13 **οὐ…ὁ ἀγὼν…ὑμῖν:** *you are not
contending;* supply ἐστί w/ ἀγών
ἀπὸ τοῦ ἴσου: *on equal footing;*
i.e. from a position of equal power
μὴ αἰσχύνην ὀφλεῖν: *so as not to
incur disgrace;* ὀφλεῖν aor. inf. <
ὀφλισκάνω, explaining ἀνδραγαθίας

14 **ἡ βουλή:** supply ἐστί.
πρὸς: *against*

15 **πολλῷ:** *greatly* (lit. *by much*); dat. of
degree of difference w/ κρείσσονας
μὴ ἀνθίστασθαι: *not to resist;* aor.
mid. inf. < ἀνθίστημι; the inf. explains σωτηρίας.

16 **τὰ τῶν πολέμων:** *war* (lit. *matters
of wars*); n. acc. pl. subj. of ind. state.,
w/ ἐπιστάμεθα
ἔστιν ὅτε: *sometimes*

17 **κοινοτέρας τὰς τύχας λαμβάνοντα ἢ κατὰ τὸ διαφέρον ἑκατέρων πλῆθος:** *allows more impartial
fortune(s) than (can be determined by)
the different size of the forces on each
side;* i.e. success in war is not always a
matter of superior power; λαμβάνοντα, ppl. in ind. state. (w/ ἐπιστάμεθα), agrees w/ τὰ τῶν πολέμων,
acc. subj. of ind. statement

18 **τὸ μὲν εἶξαι:** *to submit;* art. inf., subj.
of implied ἐστί
εὐθὺς: *straightway;* adv.
ἀνέλπιστον: *despair;* lit. *hopeless* or
a hopeless matter

19 **μετὰ δὲ τοῦ δρωμένου:** *with action;*
δρωμένου, pres. mid. (or pass.) ppl. <
δράω
στῆναι…ὀρθῶς: *(of) standing
upright;* i.e. of surviving; στῆναι, aor.
act. inf. < ἵστημι, w/ ἐλπίς; the phrase
στῆναι ὀρθῶς may also suggest standing tall as brave men in battle.
ἐλπὶς: supply ἐστι.

ἅμα: at the same time; along with (dat.)

ἀνα-ρριπτω: to toss up (dice); run a risk

ἀνθρώπειος, -α, -ον: human

ἀ-σθενής, -ές: weak, feeble, sick

ἀ-φανής, ές: unseen, unnoticed

βλάπτω: to harm, hurt, damage

γνωρίζω: to make known, gain knowledge of

δάπανος, -ον: extravagant, lavish

ἐάν (εἰ ἄν, ἤν): if

εἷς, μία, ἕν: one, single, alone

ἐλ-λείπω: to fall short, lack; leave behind

ἐπειδάν: whenever

ἐπι-λείπω: to leave behind; fail, be wanting

καθ-αιρέω (aor. -εῖλον): to take down (by force), destroy

καθ-ίστημι: to set up, establish; to become, bring into a certain state

κίνδυνος, ὁ: risk, danger, venture

λυμαίνομαι: to outrage, maltreat; cause ruin

μαντικός, -ή, -όν: prophetic; prophetic (art)

μηδέ: and not, but not, nor

ὁμοιόω: to make like, assimilate; be like

ὅστις, ἥτις, ὅ τι: who-, which-, whatever

παρα-μύθιον, τό: encouragement, exhortation; an abatement, assuagement, consolation

πάρ-ειμι: to be near, be present; (impersonal) to be in one's power

περι-ουσία ἡ: surplus, abundance; advantage

πιέζω: to press, weigh down, squeeze

ῥοπή, ἡ: weighing or turn (of a scale); weight

σφάλλω: to make fall, overthrow, defeat; frustrate; (pass.) be overthrown; go wrong, be frustrated, be mistaken in something (gen.)

σῴζω: to save, keep, preserve

τοιοῦτος, -αύτη, -οῦτο: such

ὑπ-άρχω: to be there, exist, be ready, be available

φανερός, -ά, -όν: visible, manifest, evident

φυλάσσω: to guard; (mid.) to guard against

φύσις, -εως, ἡ: nature, character

χράομαι: to use, employ, engage in (dat.)

χρησμός, ὁ: oracle, oracular response

ΑΘ. Ἐλπὶς δὲ κινδύνῳ παραμύθιον οὖσα τοὺς μὲν ἀπὸ   103
περιουσίας χρωμένους αὐτῇ, κἂν βλάψῃ, οὐ καθεῖλεν· τοῖς
δ' ἐς ἄπαν τὸ ὑπάρχον ἀναρριπτοῦσι (δάπανος γὰρ φύσει)
ἅμα τε γιγνώσκεται σφαλέντων καὶ ἐν ὅτῳ ἔτι φυλάξεταί
τις αὐτὴν γνωρισθεῖσαν οὐκ ἐλλείπει. ὃ ὑμεῖς ἀσθενεῖς τε
καὶ ἐπὶ ῥοπῆς μιᾶς ὄντες μὴ βούλεσθε παθεῖν μηδὲ ὁμοιωθῆ-   25
ναι τοῖς πολλοῖς, οἷς παρὸν ἀνθρωπείως ἔτι σῴζεσθαι, ἐπειδὰν πιεζομένους αὐτοὺς ἐπιλίπωσιν αἱ φανεραὶ ἐλπίδες, ἐπὶ
τὰς ἀφανεῖς καθίστανται μαντικήν τε καὶ χρησμοὺς καὶ
ὅσα τοιαῦτα μετ' ἐλπίδων λυμαίνεται.

---

20 **Ἐλπὶς δὲ**: echoes ἐλπὶς in 5.102
παραμύθιον οὖσα: *which is encourag-*
ment (for risk), or *solace (in danger)*
τοὺς μὲν...χρωμένους: *those having*
recourse to; dir. obj. of βλάψῃ and καθεῖλεν; pres. ppl. < χράομαι
αὐτῇ: *it*; i.e. hope; dat. w/ χράομαι
ἀπὸ περιουσίας: *when there is plenty*;
i.e. when they can afford to lose

21 **κἂν βλάψῃ**: κἂν = καὶ ἂν, w/ aor.
subjunct.
οὐ καθεῖλεν: *does not utterly ruin*; a
gnomic aor. (stating a general truth)
< καθαιρέω; translate as pres.
τοῖς δ' ἐς ἄπαν τὸ ὑπάρχον ἀναρ-
ριπτοῦσι: *but for men who risk all they*
have at a toss (of the dice); ἀναρριπτοῦσι dat. pl. ppl.

23 **γιγνώσκεται**: *it is known* or *recognized*;
i.e. for what it truly is
σφαλέντων: *when (all) has gone*
wrong; n. pl. aor. pass. ppl. in gen. abs.;
possibly m. pl., referring to τοῖς ἀναρριπτοῦσι (despite the case)
ἐν ὅτῳ...οὐκ ἐλλείπει: *and it does*
not leave room for someone to guard
against it in the future, after it is
known; ἐν ὅτῳ = *(a place) in which*;
i.e. an opportunity to

24 **αὐτὴν**: *it*; i.e. hope; dir. obj. of
φυλάξεται
γνωρισθεῖσαν: *when recognized (for*
what it is); aor. pass. ppl. < γνωρίζω
ὃ...μὴ βούλεσθε παθεῖν: *do not let*
this happen to you; παθεῖν, aor. inf. <
πάσχω

25 **ἐπὶ ῥοπῆς μιᾶς ὄντες**: *when your fate*
depends on a single turn (of a scale); i.e.
the scale is about to tip
μηδὲ ὁμοιωθῆναι: *and do not become*
like; aor. pass. inf. also w/ μὴ βούλεσθε

26 **τοῖς πολλοῖς**: dat. w/ ὁμοιωθῆναι; to
suggest to "the few" that they may
become like "the many" is an insult.
οἷς παρὸν: *although they are able*;
n. acc. ppl. < πάρειμι, in acc. abs. w/
subj. in dat.; οἷς refers to τοῖς πολλοῖς
ἀνθρωπείως: *by human means*
σῴζεσθαι: inf. w/ παρὸν

27 **ἐπειδὰν πιεζομένους αὐτοὺς ἐπι-**
λίπωσιν αἱ φανεραὶ ἐλπίδες: *when-*
ever manifest (i.e. well-founded) hopes
abandon them, as they are being
pressed down (by misfortune)
ἐπὶ τὰς ἀφανεῖς καθίστανται: *they*
turn to insubstantial (hopes)

29 **καὶ ὅσα τοιαῦτα λυμαίνεται**: n. pl.
subj. w/ sg. verb

ἀγωνίζομαι: to contend, compete, fight
αἰσχύνη, ἡ: shame, disgrace, dishonor
ἄ-λογος, -ον: without speech; contrary to reason
ἀνάγκη, ἡ: necessity, force, constraint
βοηθέω: to come to aid, assist, aid
βούλησις, -εως, ἡ: wish, will; purpose
δύναμις, -εως, ἡ: power, force, capacity
ἐλασσόω: to lessen; (pass.) to suffer loss, be inferior, be at a disadvantage
ἐλ-λείπω: to fall short, lack; leave behind
ἕνεκα: for the sake of, because of (gen.)
ἔξω: out of (gen.); adv. outside
εὐ-μένεια, ἡ: favor, goodwill
θρασύνω: to embolden, encourage
νόμισις, -εως, ἡ: belief, opinion
ξυγ-γένεια, ἡ: kinship, family
ξυμ-μαχία, ἡ: an alliance
οἶδα: to know
ὅμως: nevertheless, however, yet
ὅσιος, -α, -ον: holy; pious, religious; righteous, lawful
οὐ-δέ: and not, but not, nor, not even
οὐδ-είς, οὐδε-μία, οὐδ-έν: no one, nothing
οὕτως: in this way, thus, so
παντά-πασι: all in all, altogether, entirely
πιστεύω: to trust, believe in, rely on
πρόσ-ειμι (εἰμί): to be in addition, be added to; to be present
σφεῖς: they
τοί-νυν: well then; therefore, accordingly
ὑμέτερος, -α, -ον: your, yours
χαλεπός, -ά, -όν: difficult, hard, harmful

ΜΗΛ. Χαλεπὸν μὲν καὶ ἡμεῖς (εὖ ἴστε) νομίζομεν πρὸς 104
δύναμίν τε τὴν ὑμετέραν καὶ τὴν τύχην, εἰ μὴ ἀπὸ τοῦ 1
ἴσου ἔσται, ἀγωνίζεσθαι· ὅμως δὲ πιστεύομεν τῇ μὲν τύχῃ
ἐκ τοῦ θείου μὴ ἐλασσώσεσθαι, ὅτι ὅσιοι πρὸς οὐ δικαίους
ἱστάμεθα, τῆς δὲ δυνάμεως τῷ ἐλλείποντι τὴν Λακεδαιμονίων
ἡμῖν ξυμμαχίαν προσέσεσθαι, ἀνάγκην ἔχουσαν, καὶ εἰ μή του 5
ἄλλου, τῆς γε ξυγγενείας ἕνεκα καὶ αἰσχύνῃ βοηθεῖν. καὶ
οὐ παντάπασιν οὕτως ἀλόγως θρασυνόμεθα.

ΑΘ. Τῆς μὲν τοίνυν πρὸς τὸ θεῖον εὐμενείας οὐδ' ἡμεῖς 105
οἰόμεθα λελείψεσθαι· οὐδὲν γὰρ ἔξω τῆς ἀνθρωπείας τῶν μὲν
ἐς τὸ θεῖον νομίσεως, τῶν δ' ἐς σφᾶς αὐτοὺς βουλήσεως 10

---

30 **Χαλεπὸν...νομίζομεν:** supply εἶναι
καὶ ἡμεῖς: *we, too*
ἴστε: imper. 2p < οἶδα
1 **εἰ μὴ ἀπὸ τοῦ ἴσου ἔσται:** *if the contest is not on equal terms;* infer ἀγών from ἀγωνίζεσθαι; an emotional fut. cond. w/ fut. indic. expressing fear
3 **ἀγωνίζεσθαι:** inf. w/ χαλεπὸν (εἶναι)
τῇ μὲν τύχῃ: dat. w/ πιστεύομεν
4 **ἐκ τοῦ θείου:** *divine;* lit. *from the divine;* i.e. from the gods
μὴ ἐλασσώσεσθαι: *that we will not have the worst of it;* i.e. suffer a loss or be defeated; fut. inf., w/ πιστεύομεν
ὅσιοι: *as righteous men*
ἱστάμεθα: *we (take our) stand*
τῷ ἐλλείποντι: *our deficiency;* dat. w/ προσέσεσθαι
5 **προσέσεσθαι:** *will compensate for;* inf. w/ πιστεύομεν
τὴν...ξυμμαχίαν: *the Lacs.' alliance;* acc. subj. of προσέσεσθαι; the position of ἡμῖν suggests *the alliance with us,* a puzzling statement, but perhaps referring to a future alliance.
ἀνάγκην ἔχουσαν: *since it [the alliance] is under obligation (to act)*

καὶ εἰ μὴ του ἄλλου: *even if for no other (reason);* gen. w/ ἕνεκα
6 **τῆς ξυγγενείας ἕνεκα καὶ αἰσχύνῃ:** *because of our kinship and from a sense of shame;* i.e. to avoid disgrace
βοηθεῖν: inf. w/ ἀνάγκην ἔχουσαν
7 **οὐ παντάπασιν:** *not entirely*
8 **τῆς...πρὸς τὸ θεῖον εὐμενείας:** *in regard to divine good will* or *to the favour of the gods,* gen. w/ λελείψεσθαι
οὐδ' ἡμεῖς οἰόμεθα λελείψεσθαι: *we also* (i.e. like you) *do not think we will be found wanting;* λελείψεσθαι fut. perf. pass. inf. of ἐλλείπω
9 **οὐδὲν:** dir. obj. of δικαιοῦμεν ἢ πράσσομεν (p. 31)
ἔξω τῆς ἀνθρωπείας...νομίσεως: *beyond mens' usual belief and practice*
τῶν μὲν ἐς τὸ θεῖον: *(as far as) what has to do with the gods* (lit. *the divine*); the gen. limits νομίσεως.
10 **τῶν δ' ἐς σφᾶς αὐτοὺς:** *and (as far as) what pertains to themselves;* the gen. limits βουλήσεως.
βουλήσεως: *(beyond what men) want* or *intend;* second obj. of ἔξω; supply ἀνθρωπείας.

αἰσχρός, -ά, -όν: shameful, disgraceful

ἀναγκαῖος, -α, -ον: necessary, inevitable

ἀνθρώπειος, -α, -ον: human

ἀ-πειρό-κακος, -ον: without experience of evil, ignorant of evil

βοηθέω: to come to aid, assist, aid

δή: indeed, surely, really, certainly, just

δικαιόω: to deem right, think right

δόξα, ἡ: expectation, reputation, opinion

δράω: to do, act

δύναμις, -εως, ἡ: power, force, capacity

εἰκός, -ότος, τό: likelihood, what is likely, probable, reasonable (neut. pf.
    ppl. < ἔοικα)

ἐλασσόω: to lessen; (pass.) to suffer loss, be inferior, be at a disadvantage

ἡγέομαι: to lead; consider, think, believe

θεῖος, -α, -ον: divine, sent by the gods

κατα-λείπω: to leave behind, abandon

κεῖμαι: to lie, lie down; to be laid down, established (as in laws)

κρατέω: to be strong; conquer, prevail

μακαρίζω: to deem blessed or happy

οὗ: where

οὔ-τε: and not; οὔτε…οὔτε: neither…nor

οὕτως: in this way, thus, so

παρα-λαμβάνω: to receive, to inherit

πιστεύω: to trust, believe in, rely on

σαφής, -ές: clear, distinct, definite

φύσις, -εως, ἡ: nature, character

χράομαι: to use, employ, engage in (dat.)

δικαιοῦμεν ἢ πράσσομεν. ἡγούμεθα γὰρ τό τε θεῖον δόξῃ
τὸ ἀνθρώπειόν τε σαφῶς διὰ παντὸς ὑπὸ φύσεως ἀναγκαίας,
οὗ ἂν κρατῇ, ἄρχειν· καὶ ἡμεῖς οὔτε θέντες τὸν νόμον οὔτε
κειμένῳ πρῶτοι χρησάμενοι, ὄντα δὲ παραλαβόντες καὶ
ἐσόμενον ἐς αἰεὶ καταλείψοντες χρώμεθα αὐτῷ, εἰδότες καὶ 15
ὑμᾶς ἂν καὶ ἄλλους ἐν τῇ αὐτῇ δυνάμει ἡμῖν γενομένους
δρῶντας ἂν ταὐτό. καὶ πρὸς μὲν τὸ θεῖον οὕτως ἐκ τοῦ
εἰκότος οὐ φοβούμεθα ἐλασσώσεσθαι· τῆς δὲ ἐς Λακεδαιμονίους δόξης, ἣν διὰ τὸ αἰσχρὸν δὴ βοηθήσειν ὑμῖν
πιστεύετε αὐτούς, μακαρίσαντες ὑμῶν τὸ ἀπειρόκακον οὐ 20

---

11 **δίκαιοῦμεν ἢ πράσσομεν:** *we deem right and do;* w/ dir. obj. οὐδεν (p. 29)
τό θεῖον: *the gods;* lit. *the divine* acc. subj. of inf. ἄρχειν in ind. state.
δόξῃ: *in point of opinion;* vs. σαφῶς, what we see clearly before us

12 **τὸ ἀνθρώπειόν τε:** *and men* (lit. *the human*)
διὰ παντός: *always* or *in all matters*
ὑπὸ φύσεως ἀναγκαίας: *by an irresistible (law of) nature*

13 **οὗ ἂν κρατῇ:** *wherever (each) pre-vails;* ἄν + subjunct. in general cond.
καὶ ἡμεῖς οὔτε θέντες τὸν νόμον: *and neither did we establish the custom;* θέντες, m. nom. pl. aor. ppl. < τίθημι
οὔτε θέντες…οὔτε…χρησάμενοι: both neg. ppls. contrast with the pos. ppls. προλαβόντες and καταλείψ-οντες stating what the Aths. have done and expect to do.

14 **κειμένῳ:** *established;* understand τῷ νόμῳ; dat. ppl. w/ χρησάμενοι < χράομαι
ὄντα: *(already) in existence;* i.e. τὸν νόμον; dir. obj. of παραλαβόντες

15 **ἐσόμενον ἐς αἰεὶ:** *to continue forever;* fut. mid. ppl. < εἰμι; also refers to τὸν νόμον
αὐτῷ: *it;* i.e. τῷ νόμῳ; dat. w/ χρώμεθα < χράομαι

16 **ὑμᾶς…ἄλλους:** acc. subjs. of δρῶντας in ind. state. w/ εἰδότες
ἂν: appears early to warn of the mood of the ppl. δρῶντας (w/ repeated ἄν) standing for a pot. opt.
τῇ αὐτῇ δυνάμει ἡμῖν: *in the same (position of) power we are in*

17 **δρῶντας ἂν ταὐτό:** *would do the same;* ταὐτό = τὸ αὐτό
πρὸς μὲν τὸ θεῖον: *as for the gods*
ἐκ τοῦ εἰκότος: *in (all) likelihood*

18 **ἐλασσώσεσθαι:** *we will be at a disadvantage;* inf. w/ οὐ φοβούμεθα
τῆς δὲ ἐς Λακεδαιμονίους δόξης: *of your opinion of the Spartans;* gen. w/ τὸ ἀπειρόκακον

29 **ἣν:** *regarding which;* possibly accus. of respect (referring to δόξης); the true reading may be ᾗ, *whereby.*

20 **αὐτούς:** subj. of βοηθήσειν
μακαρίσαντες: note the irony.
ὑμῶν τὸ ἀπειρόκακον: *your (optimistic) naiveté* (lit. *lack of experience of evil*)

ἄ-λογος, -ον: without speech; contrary to reason

ἄ-πιστος, -ον: not trustworthy, unreliable; not trusting

ἄπ-οικος, ὁ: colonist, settler

ἄ-φρων, -ον: senseless, foolish, silly

δηλόω: to make clear, show, reveal

διάνοια, ἡ: thought, intention, purpose

Ἕλλην, Ἕλληνος, ὁ: a Greek

ἐπι-φανής, -ές: manifest, evident

ἐπι-χώριος, -α, -ον: local, native

εὔ-νους, -ουν: well-disposed to, kind to

ζηλόω: to envy, be jealous; vie with

ἡδύς, -εῖα, -ύ: pleasant; pleasing

καθ-ίστημι: to set up, establish; to become, bring into a certain state

καίτοι: and yet, and indeed, and further

μάλιστα: most of all; certainly, especially; (with numbers) approximately

νόμιμος, -η, -ον: customary

νῦν: now; as it is

ξυμ-φέρω: to bring together; to come to terms, agree; (of events) to happen; to confer a benefit, be useful, be expedient

ξυν-αιρέω (aor. ξυνεῖλον): to grasp, take together

πιστεύω: to trust, believe in, rely on

πλεῖστος, -η, -ον: most, very many

πολέμιος, -α, -ον: hostile, of the enemy

προ-δίδωμι: to betray, give over

προσ-φέρω: to bring upon, deal with, attack

σφεῖς: they

σωτηρία, ἡ: deliverance, safety

τοιοῦτος, -αύτη, -οῦτο: such

ὑμέτερος, -α, -ον: your, yours

χράομαι: to use, employ, engage in (dat)

ὠφέλιμος, -α, -ον: useful, beneficial

ζηλοῦμεν τὸ ἄφρον. Λακεδαιμόνιοι γὰρ πρὸς σφᾶς μὲν
αὐτοὺς καὶ τὰ ἐπιχώρια νόμιμα πλεῖστα ἀρετῇ χρῶνται·
πρὸς δὲ τοὺς ἄλλους πολλὰ ἄν τις ἔχων εἰπεῖν ὡς προσφέρονται, ξυνελὼν μάλιστ' ἂν δηλώσειεν ὅτι ἐπιφανέστατα
ὧν ἴσμεν τὰ μὲν ἡδέα καλὰ νομίζουσι, τὰ δὲ ξυμφέροντα   25
δίκαια.   καίτοι οὐ πρὸς τῆς ὑμετέρας νῦν ἀλόγου σωτηρίας ἡ
τοιαύτη διάνοια.

ΜΗΛ.   Ἡμεῖς δὲ κατ' αὐτὸ τοῦτο ἤδη καὶ μάλιστα   106
πιστεύομεν τῷ ξυμφέροντι αὐτῶν, Μηλίους ἀποίκους ὄντας
μὴ βουλήσεσθαι προδόντας τοῖς μὲν εὔνοις τῶν Ἑλλήνων   30
ἀπίστους καταστῆναι, τοῖς δὲ πολεμίοις ὠφελίμους.

---

22 **τὰ ἐπιχώρια νόμιμα:** *their customs
at home*
πλεῖστα ἀρετῇ χρῶνται: *act most
nobly*, or *honorably*; πλεῖστα, n. pl.
adj. used as adv.

23 **πολλὰ ἄν τις ἔχων εἰπεῖν:** *one
could say much (about)*; ἔχειν w/ inf.
= *to be able*; ἄν w/ ppl. to express
potential
ὡς προσφέρονται: *how they behave*

24 **ξυνελὼν:** *in short*; m. nom. sg. aor.
ppl. < ξυναιρέω
μάλιστα ἂν δηλώσειεν: *he would
make most clear*; aor. opt. 3s, w/ ἂν =
pot. opt.; *he* = τις of l. 24
ἐπιφανέστατα: n. pl. superl. adj.
used as adv. w/ νομίζουσι

25 **ὧν ἴσμεν:** *of those we know*
τὰ ἡδέα καλὰ νομίζουσι: *they
believe the pleasant (is) noble* (or
honorable); i.e. they equate the
pleasant with the noble; καλὰ is
pred. adj.; supply εἶναι.

26 **δίκαια:** pred. adj. w/ τὰ ξυμφέροντα; i.e. they equate the
advantageous with the just
οὐ πρὸς: *not to the advantage of*

**τῆς ὑμετέρας νῦν ἀλόγου σωτηρ-
ίας:** *your current unreasonable
(expectation of) survival*; gen. w/ πρός

27 **ἡ τοιαύτη διάνοια:** *such thinking*

28 **κατ' αὐτὸ τοῦτο ἤδη καί:** *for this
same (reason) now, in fact*; i.e. now
that we are on this topic

29 **τῷ ξυμφέροντι αὐτῶν:** *their
advantage*; dat. w/ πιστεύομεν
Μηλίους: dir. obj. of προδόντας

30 **μὴ βουλήσεσθαι προδόντας:** *that
they will not, by betraying*; inf. w/
πιστεύομεν; supply αὐτοὺς from
αὐτῶν (l. 29); the inf. clause explains
the advantage.
τοῖς μὲν εὔνοις: dat. w/ ἀπίστους
τῶν Ἑλλήνων: part. gen. w/ τοῖς
εὔνοις; i.e. those (of the) Greeks who
are well-disposed toward them

31 **ἀπίστους καταστῆναι:** *make
(themselves) untrustworthy*; καταστῆναι, aor. inf. < καθίστημι; inf. w/
μὴ βουλήσεσθαι
τοῖς δὲ πολεμίοις: dat. w/ ὠφελίμους
ὠφελίμους: supply καταστῆναι.

ἀ-σφάλεια, ἡ: security, assurance

βέβαιος, -α, -ον: steadfast, steady, firm

γνώμη, ἡ: judgment, resolve, opinion

δράω: to do, act

ἐγγύς: near (gen.); adv. nearby

ἐγ-χειρίζω: to entrust; take in hand

ἕνεκα: for the sake of, because of (gen.)

ἐπι-καλέω: to call upon, summon

ἕτερος, -α, -ον: one of two, other, different

εὔ-νους, -ουν: well disposed to, kind to

ἐχυρός, -ά, -όν: strong, secure

ἡγέομαι: to lead; consider, think, believe

ἥκιστος, -η, -ον: least; not at all

ἤν (ἐάν, εἰ ἂν): if, if ever

κεῖμαι: to lie, lie down; to be laid down, established (as in laws)

κίνδυνος, ὁ: risk, danger, venture

μᾶλλον: more, rather

μετά: with (gen.); after (acc.)

ξυγ-γενής, -ές: akin to, kindred; of like kind

ξυμ-φέρω: to bring together; to come to terms, agree; (of events) to happen;
    to confer a benefit, be useful, be expedient

ξυν-αγωνίζομαι: to contend or fight alongside

οὔκ-ουν: certainly not, and so not

Πελοπόννησος, ἡ: the Peloponnese

πιστός, -ή, -όν: trustworthy, loyal; credible

τολμάω: to dare, undertake, endure

ΑΘ.   Οὔκουν οἴεσθε τὸ ξυμφέρον μὲν μετ' ἀσφαλείας εἶναι,   107
τὸ δὲ δίκαιον καὶ καλὸν μετὰ κινδύνου δρᾶσθαι· ὃ
Λακεδαιμόνιοι ἥκιστα ὡς ἐπὶ τὸ πολὺ τολμῶσιν.

ΜΗΛ.   Ἀλλὰ καὶ τοὺς κινδύνους τε ἡμῶν ἕνεκα μᾶλλον   108
ἡγούμεθ' ἂν ἐγχειρίσασθαι αὐτούς, καὶ βεβαιοτέρους ἢ ἐς   5
ἄλλους νομιεῖν, ὅσῳ πρὸς μὲν τὰ ἔργα τῆς Πελοποννήσου
ἐγγὺς κείμεθα, τῆς δὲ γνώμης τῷ ξυγγενεῖ πιστότεροι ἑτέρων
ἐσμέν.

ΑΘ.   Τὸ δ' ἐχυρόν γε τοῖς ξυναγωνιουμένοις οὐ τὸ   109
εὔνουν τῶν ἐπικαλεσαμένων φαίνεται, ἀλλ' ἢν τῶν ἔργων   10

---

1 **Οὔκουν οἴεσθε:** *So, you do not think;*
they express incredulity.
τὸ ξυμφέρον...εἶναι: *advantage is;*
i.e. means
μετ' ἀσφαλείας: *(acting) safely*

2 **τὸ δίκαιον καὶ καλὸν:** *what is just
and noble;* obj. of δρᾶσθαι
μετὰ κινδύνου: *(comes) with risk*
δρᾶσθαι: *to do;* pres. mid. inf. in ind.
state. w/ οἴεσθε
ὃ: *this;* i.e. undertaking risk; dir. obj. of
τολμῶσιν

3 **ἥκιστα:** *least;* n. pl. as adv.
ὡς ἐπὶ τὸ πολὺ: *generally*

4 **Ἀλλὰ καὶ:** *to the contrary, in fact*
τοὺς κινδύνους: dir. obj. of ἐγχειρίσασθαι

5 **ἂν ἐγχειρίσασθαι αὐτούς:** *they
would undertake;* acc. / inf. w/ ἂν
expressing pot. in ind. state. w/
ἡγούμεθ'
βεβαιοτέρους: *involving more certain
outcomes;* supply κινδύνους
ἢ ἐς ἄλλους: *than for others*

6 **νομιεῖν:** *they will believe;* fut. inf.
< νομίζω, in ind. state.; supply subj.
αὐτούς.
ὅσῳ: *inasmuch as*

πρὸς τὰ ἔργα: *when it comes to
action;* i.e. military operations
τῆς Πελοποννήσου: gen. w/ ἔγγυς,
or w/ τὰ ἔργα (*the affairs of the Pel.*),
with ἔγγυς as adv. w/ κείμεθα

7 **κείμεθα:** *we lie,* or *we are situated*
τῆς δὲ γνώμης τῷ ξυγγενεῖ: *because of our affinity of view(s);* there is
no consensus about the syntax: τῆς
γνώμης w/ πιστότεροι (*more depend-
able of thought*) or w/ dat. τῷ ξυγγενεῖ (*because of kinship*)? Some
suggest emending to τὴν γνώμην (acc.
of respect), which seems unnecessary
given the flexibility of the gen.; see
ἀπιστίᾳ w/ gen. in 5.109.

9 **Τὸ δ' ἐχυρόν:** *strength;* subj. of
φαίνεται
φαίνεται: *is seen (as consisting of)*
τοῖς ξυναγωνιουμένοις: *for those
who intend to join the fight;* fut. ppl.
**οὐ τὸ εὔνουν τῶν ἐπικαλεσα-
μένων:** *not the good will of those
who summon (their aid);* pred. nom.
w/ τὸ δ' ἐχυρόν φαίνεται

10 **ἀλλ' ἢν:** this cond. is the second pred.
nom. of τὸ δ' ἐχυρόν φαίνεται,
defining what security is vs. what it is
not (τὸ εὔνουν).

ἀπιστία, ἡ: disbelief, distrust, mistrust

ἄ-πορος, -ον: difficult, impracticable

Βρασίδας, ὁ: Brasidas, an enterprising Spartan commander who spawned revolts among Athens' allies in the Thraceward region and opposed making peace. Along with the Athenian general and politician Cleon, also opposed to peace, he was killed at the battle of Amphipolis in 422.

γοῦν: γε οὖν, at least, at any rate, anyway

δύναμις, -εως, ἡ: power, force, capacity

εἰκός, -ότος, τό: likelihood, what is likely, probable, reasonable (neut. pf. ppl. < ἔοικα)

ἐπ-έρχομαι: to come upon; attack

κρατέω: to be strong; conquer, prevail

Κρητικός, -η, -ον: from Crete, Cretan

λανθάνω: to escape notice of, act unnoticed

λῆψις, -εως, ἡ: seizure

λοιπός, -ή, -όν: remaining, the rest

μᾶλλον: more, rather

μετά: with (gen.); after (acc.)

ναυ-κράτωρ, ὁ: master of the sea, (lit.) master of a ship

νῆσος, ἡ: an island

ξυμ-μαχίς, -ίδος: allied (fem. of adj. ξύμμαχος)

ὅδε, ἥδε, τόδε: this

οἰκεῖος, -α, -ον: intimate, close, related

παρασκευή, ἡ: preparation; intrigue

πέλαγος, τό: sea

πέλας: near

περαιόω: to cross

πλέων, -ον: more, greater

πόνος, ὁ: work, toil

προ-έχω: to hold forth; be first, surpass, excel

προσ-ήκω: to have come, be present; belong to, be befitting or proper

σκοπέω: to look at, examine, consider

σφάλλω: to make fall, overthrow, defeat; frustrate; (pass.) be overthrown; go wrong, be frustrated, be mistaken in something (gen.)

σωτηρία, ἡ: deliverance, safety

ὥστε: so that, that, so as to, and so

τις δυνάμει πολὺ προύχῃ· ὃ Λακεδαιμόνιοι καὶ πλέον τι τῶν ἄλλων σκοποῦσιν (τῆς γοῦν οἰκείας παρασκευῆς ἀπιστίᾳ καὶ μετὰ ξυμμάχων πολλῶν τοῖς πέλας ἐπέρχονται), ὥστε οὐκ εἰκὸς ἐς νῆσόν γε αὐτοὺς ἡμῶν ναυκρατόρων ὄντων περαιωθῆναι. 15

ΜΗΛ. Οἱ δὲ καὶ ἄλλους ἂν ἔχοιεν πέμψαι· πολὺ δὲ τὸ 110 Κρητικὸν πέλαγος, δι' οὗ τῶν κρατούντων ἀπορώτερος ἡ λῆψις ἢ τῶν λαθεῖν βουλομένων ἡ σωτηρία. καὶ εἰ τοῦδε σφάλλοιντο, τράποιντ' ἂν καὶ ἐς τὴν γῆν ὑμῶν καὶ ἐπὶ τοὺς λοιποὺς τῶν ξυμμάχων, ὅσους μὴ Βρασίδας ἐπῆλθεν· καὶ 20 οὐ περὶ τῆς μὴ προσηκούσης μᾶλλον ἢ τῆς οἰκειοτέρας ξυμμαχίδος τε καὶ γῆς ὁ πόνος ὑμῖν ἔσται.

---

11 **τις...πολὺ προύχῃ:** *someone is far superior*; pres. subjunct. of προέχω w/ ἤν (p. 35) in a general statement
δυνάμει: *in (physical) power*; w/ ἔργων (p. 35)
ὃ: *this factor*, i.e. someone's strength
καὶ πλέον τι: *even somewhat more*
τῶν ἄλλων: gen. of comp. w/ πλέον

12 **γοῦν:** *at least*; provides partial proof

13 **τοῖς πέλας:** *their neighbors*; lit. *those nearby*; dat. w/ ἐπέρχονται

14 **γε:** emphasizes νῆσον; Melos not only is farther away than most places Sparta attacks, but also is accessible only by sea.
ἡμῶν ναυκρατόρων ὄντων: gen. abs.

15 **περαιωθῆναι:** *cross over*; aor. pass., but mid. in sense

16 **ἂν ἔχοιεν:** *they would be able*; pot. opt.
πολὺ: *is vast*; supply ἐστι.

17 **δι' οὗ:** *on account of which*; i.e. the size of the sea
κρατούντων: *by those controlling*;

subjective gen. w/ λῆψις; i.e. those in control will have difficulty seizing men running the blockade.
ἀπορώτερος: two-ending adj. modifying λῆψις

18 **τῶν λαθεῖν βουλομένων:** *of those wanting to elude them*; objective gen. w/ σωτηρία
τοῦδε: *in this (effort)*; gen. w/ σφάλλοιντο

20 **ὅσους μὴ Βρασίδας ἐπῆλθεν:** *however many (allies) Brasidas did not approach*

21 **οὐ...μᾶλλον ἢ:** "not x more than y" means "y as much as, if not more than, x."
περὶ τῆς μὴ προσηκούσης: *for land not belonging to you*
τῆς οἰκειοτέρας ξυμμαχίδος τε καὶ γῆς: *for your own land and for that of your allies*; the sense is clear, but the syntax is not; καὶ should perhaps be bracketed.

22 **ὁ πόνος ὑμῖν ἔσται:** *you will have to struggle*

ἀν-επιστήμων, -ον: unskilled, ignorant
ἄνθρωπος, ὁ: human being
ἀντι-τάσσω: to arrange against, set opposite
ἀπό: from, away from (gen.)
ἀπο-χωρέω: to go from, depart, withdraw
βουλεύω: to deliberate, plan, take counsel
βραχύς, -έα, -ύ: short
εἷς, μία, ἕν: one, single, alone
ἐλπίζω: to hope for, look for, expect
ἐν-θυμέομαι: to take to heart, consider, ponder
ἰσχυρός, -ά, -όν: strong, powerful
μέλλω: to be about to, intend to
οὐ-δέ: and not, but not, nor, not even
οὐδ-είς, οὐδε-μία, οὐδ-έν: no one, nothing
πειράω: to attempt, endeavor, try
πιστεύω: to trust, believe in, rely on
πολιορκία, ἡ: a siege, blockade
πώ-ποτε: yet ever, ever
σῴζω: to save, keep, preserve
σωτηρία, ἡ: deliverance, safety
τοσοῦτος, -αύτη, -οῦτο: so (or such) great, so many, so much
ὑπ-άρχω: to be there, exist, be ready, be available

ΑΘ. Τούτων μὲν καὶ πεπειραμένοις ἄν τι γένοιτο καὶ 111
ὑμῖν καὶ οὐκ ἀνεπιστήμοσιν ὅτι οὐδ' ἀπὸ μιᾶς πώποτε
πολιορκίας Ἀθηναῖοι δι' ἄλλων φόβον ἀπεχώρησαν. ἐν- 25
θυμούμεθα δὲ ὅτι φήσαντες περὶ σωτηρίας βουλεύσειν οὐδὲν
ἐν τοσούτῳ λόγῳ εἰρήκατε ᾧ ἄνθρωποι ἂν πιστεύσαντες
νομίσειαν σωθήσεσθαι, ἀλλ' ὑμῶν τὰ μὲν ἰσχυρότατα ἐλπιζόμενα μέλλεται, τὰ δ' ὑπάρχοντα βραχέα πρὸς τὰ ἤδη

---

23 **Τούτων μὲν καὶ πεπειραμένοις ἄντι γένοιτο καὶ ὑμῖν:** *you, too, may experience something of this kind;* τούτων, part. gen. with τι, refers to the Mels.' warnings; πεπειραμένοις, pf. mid. ppl. (< πειράω); a ppl. in dat. (of interest) with εἶναι or γίγνεσθαι can be use in place of a finite verb, as in προσδεχομένῳ μοι...γέγνηται: *I expected it would happen that ...* (Thuc. 2.60.1)

24 **καὶ οὐ ἀνεπιστήμοσιν:** *and not be (left) ignorant (of the fact) that;* i.e. experience will teach them. The adj. introduces ind. state. Alternatively it could mean they think the Mels. are already aware of the Aths.' reputation.
ἀπὸ μιᾶς: *from a single*

25 **ἄλλων:** obj. gen. w/ φόβον; i.e. fear of others not others' fear
ἐνθυμούμεθα: *we see to our regret;* the verb connotes deep concern.

26 **βουλεύσειν:** supply subj. *you,* which is the subj. of εἰρήκατε
οὐδὲν: dir obj. of εἰρήκατε

27 **ἐν τοσούτῳ λόγῳ;** *in the discussion so far*
εἰρήκατε: pf. act. 2p of λέγω
ᾧ...πιστεύσαντες: *with trust in which*

28 **ἄνθρωποι ἂν...νομίσειαν:** *men... could believe;* aor. opt. 3p, w/ ἄν = pot. opt.
σωθήσεσθαι: fut. pass. inf. < σῴζω; inf. in ind. state. w/ νομίσειαν; supply the subj. *they* from ἄνθρωποι ἂν νομίσειαν.
ὑμῶν τὰ μὲν ἰσχυρότατα ἐλπιζόμενα μέλλεται: *your strongest hopes are (off in) the future;* sg. verb w/ n. pl. subj.; ἐλπιζόμενα, lit. *things hoped for*
τὰ δ' ὑπάρχοντα βραχέα: *your present resources are few;* i.e. too few; w/ explanatory inf. περιγίγνεσθαι (p. 41)
πρὸς τὰ ἤδη [ἀντιτεταγμένα]: *in face of what is already marshaled (against you);* ἀντιτεταγμένα (p. 41), pf. pass. ppl. < ἀντιτάσσω

αἰσχρός, -ά, -όν: shameful, disgraceful

αἰσχύνη, ἡ: shame, disgrace, dishonor

ἀ-λογία, ἡ: want of reason, absurdity, rashness

ἀν-ήκεστος, -ον: incurable, irreparable, fatal

ἄ-νοια, ἡ: folly, a lack of understanding

ἀντι-τάσσω: to arrange against, set opposite

ἀ-πρεπής, -ές: unseemly, improper

βουλεύω: to deliberate, plan, take counsel

δή: indeed, surely, really, certainly, just

διάνοια, ἡ: thought, intention, purpose

δια-φθείρω: to destroy utterly, disable

δύναμις, -εως, ἡ: power, force, capacity

ἑκών, ἑκοῦσα, ἑκόν: willing, intentionally

ἐπ-αγωγός, -όν: attractive, luring on

ἐπι-σπάω: to bring on; draw to, entice; persuade

ἤν (ἐάν, εἰ ἄν): if, if ever

ἡσσάομαι: to be less or weaker than, inferior to; to be defeated

κίνδυνος, ὁ: risk, danger, venture

μεθ-ίστημι: to change (place); remove

μετά: with (gen.); after (acc.)

ξυμ-φορά, ἡ: misfortune, mishap, event

ὅδε, ἥδε, τόδε: this

οἷος, -α, -ον: of what sort, as

ὄνομα, τό: name, phrase, expression

παρ-έχω: to provide, furnish, give

περι-γίγνομαι: to prevail over, be superior (to)

περι-πίπτω: to fall on, be wrecked

πλεῖστος, -η, -ον: most, very many

πρό-οπτος, -ον: foreseen, manifest

προ-οράω: to see beforehand; see before one's eyes; take thought of

προσ-λαμβάνω: to take in addition

ῥῆμα, -ατος, τό: word, saying, speech

φυλάσσω: to guard; (mid.) guard against

ἀντιτεταγμένα περιγίγνεσθαι. πολλήν τε ἀλογίαν τῆς 1
διανοίας παρέχετε, εἰ μὴ μεταστησάμενοι ἔτι ἡμᾶς ἄλλο τι
τῶνδε σωφρονέστερον γνώσεσθε. οὐ γὰρ δὴ ἐπί γε τὴν ἐν
τοῖς αἰσχροῖς καὶ προύπτοις κινδύνοις πλεῖστα διαφθείρουσαν
ἀνθρώπους αἰσχύνην τρέψεσθε. πολλοῖς γὰρ προορωμένοις 5
ἔτι ἐς οἷα φέρονται τὸ αἰσχρὸν καλούμενον ὀνόματος ἐπαγωγοῦ δυνάμει ἐπεσπάσατο ἡσσηθεῖσι τοῦ ῥήματος ἔργῳ
ξυμφοραῖς ἀνηκέστοις ἑκόντας περιπεσεῖν καὶ αἰσχύνην
αἰσχίω μετὰ ἀνοίας ἢ τύχῃ προσλαβεῖν. ὃ ὑμεῖς, ἢν εὖ
βουλεύησθε, φυλάξεσθε, καὶ οὐκ ἀπρεπὲς νομιεῖτε πόλεώς τε 10

---

1 **περιγίγνεσθαι:** *to prevail,* or *for success;* inf. explains βραχέα (p. 39)
πολλήν τε ἀλογίαν τῆς διανοίας παρέχετε: *and you show how very foolish (or rash) you are;* lit. *show much lack of thought*

2 **εἰ μὴ...ἔτι...γνώσεσθε:** *if you still do not come to a decision;* εἰ w/ fut. indic. to warn
μεταστησάμενοι...ἡμᾶς: i.e. to confer privately

3 **τῶνδε:** gen. of comp. w/ ἄλλο τι... σωφρονέστερον
οὐ γὰρ δὴ...τρέψεσθε: *for of course you will not turn to;* another warning
ἐπί γε τὴν...αἰσχύνην: *a (false) sense of shame;* i.e. a desire to preserve honor at all costs
ἐν τοῖς αἰσχροῖς καὶ προύπτοις κινδύνοις: *in dangers that are disgraceful and foreseen;* i.e. disgraceful <u>because</u> foreseen and preventable

4 **πλεῖστα:** adv. w/ ppl. διαφθείρουσαν
διαφθείρουσαν: ppl. w/ αἰσχύνην; dir. obj. is ἀνθρώπους.

5 **πολλοῖς προορωμένοις:** dat. obj. of ἐπεσπάσατο

6 **ἐς οἷα φέρονται:** *into what kinds of (dangers) they are headed*
τὸ αἰσχρὸν καλούμενον: *what is called dishonorable;* subj. of ἐπεσπάσατο
ἐπεσπάσατο: *entices;* a gnomic aor.
ὀνόματος ἐπαγωγοῦ δυνάμει: *by the power of a seductive word*

7 **ἡσσηθεῖσι τοῦ ῥήματος ἔργῳ:** *defeated by the effect of a word;* aor. pass. ppl. in dat. pl.; it modifies πολλοῖς προορωμένοις. Notice the λόγος / ἔργον antithesis.

8 **ξυμφοραῖς ἀνηκέστοις:** dat. w/ περιπεσπεσεῖν
ἑκόντας περιπεσεῖν: *to fall willingly into;* aor. inf. < περιπίπτω; inf. w/ ἐπεσπάσατο. Note the shift from dat. (ἡσσηθεῖσι) to accus. (ἑκόντας).
αἰσχύνην αἰσχίω μετὰ ἀνοίας ἢ τύχῃ προσλαβεῖν: *and to incur shame more dishonorable (since it is combined with folly) than (shame incurred) because of (mis)fortune*

9 **ὃ:** *this;* i.e. being foolishly lured by the power of a word; dir. obj. of φυλάξασθε

10 **οὐκ ἀπρεπὲς:** supply εἶναι.
πόλεώς: gen. w/ ἡσσᾶσθαι (p. 43)

αἵρεσις, -εως, ὁ: choice

ἀ-σφάλεια, ἡ: security, assurance

βουλεύω: to deliberate, plan, take counsel

εἴκω: to yield, give way, retire

εἷς, μία, ἔν: one, single, alone

ἐν-θυμέομαι: to take to heart, consider, ponder

ἡσσάομαι: to be less or weaker than, inferior to; to be defeated

ἥσσων, -ον: less, weaker, inferior

κατ-ορθόω: to set upright, erect

κρείσσων, -ον: better, stronger, superior

μέγιστος, -η, -ον: greatest, best, longest

μεθ-ίστημι: to change (place); remove

μέτριος, -α, -ον: moderate, temperate

ὀρθόω: to set straight, set upright

ὅστις, ἥτις, ὅ τι: who-, which-, whatever

οὖν: and so, then; at all events

πατρίς, -ίδος, ἡ: fatherland, land of one's forebears, native land

πλεῖστος, -η, -ον: most, very many

πολλάκις: many times, often, frequently

προ-καλέω: to call forth; to propose or offer; (mostly mid.) to provoke, challenge

προσ-φέρω: to bring upon, deal with, attack

σκοπέω: to look at, examine, consider

ὑμέτερος, -α, -ον: your, yours

ὑπο-τελής, ές: tributary, subject to tribute or taxes

φιλονικέω: to be fond of victory, contentious; obstinate

χείρων, -ον: worse, inferior

τῆς μεγίστης ἡσσᾶσθαι μέτρια προκαλουμένης, ξυμμάχους
γενέσθαι ἔχοντας τὴν ὑμετέραν αὐτῶν ὑποτελεῖς, καὶ δοθείσης αἱρέσεως πολέμου πέρι καὶ ἀσφαλείας μὴ τὰ χείρω
φιλονικῆσαι· ὡς οἵτινες τοῖς μὲν ἴσοις μὴ εἴκουσι, τοῖς δὲ
κρείσσοσι καλῶς προσφέρονται, πρὸς δὲ τοὺς ἥσσους μέτριοί
εἰσι, πλεῖστ' ἂν ὀρθοῖντο. σκοπεῖτε οὖν καὶ μεταστάντων
ἡμῶν καὶ ἐνθυμεῖσθε πολλάκις ὅτι περὶ πατρίδος βου-
λεύεσθε, ἧς μιᾶς πέρι καὶ ἐς μίαν βουλὴν τυχοῦσάν τε καὶ
μὴ κατορθώσασαν ἔσται.

15

---

11 **(πόλεως) τῆς μέγιστης ἡσσᾶσθαι:**
*to be subordinated to the most power-
ful city;* ἡσσᾶσθαι, lit. *to be made less
than;* pres. pass. infin. w/ gen. of
comp.; infin. w/ οὐκ ἀπρεπές [εἶναι]
νομιεῖτε (p. 41)
μέτρια προκαλουμένης: *(which is)
proposing moderate terms;* ppl. modifies πόλεως (p. 41)
ξυμμάχους γενέσθαι: *that you
become allies;* supply ὑμᾶς as subj. of
inf.; the phrase explains the terms
of the agreement.

12 **ἔχοντας:** modifies understood ὑμᾶς
τὴν ὑμετέραν αὐτῶν: *your own
(city);* supply πόλιν (or possibly γῆν).
ὑποτελεῖς: m. acc. pl. < ὑποτελής,
pred. adj. w/ understood ὑμᾶς
δοθείσης: gen. sg. aor. pass. ppl.
< δίδωμι w/ αἱρέσεως in gen. abs.

13 **πέρι:** the first obj. precedes the prep.;
the second (ἀσφαλείας) follows it.
μὴ τὰ χείρω φιλονικῆσαι: *not to be
obstinate for the worse;* i.e. not to be
so stubborn as to make a bad choice;
inf. w/ οὐκ ἀπρεπές [εἶναι] νομιεῖτε

14 **μὴ εἴκουσι:** μή instead of οὐκ in a
generalization w/ οἵτινες

15 **καλῶς προσφέρονται:** *behave
properly;* a euphemism for *to submit
to*

16 **πλεῖστ' ἂν ὀρθοῖντο:** *would be most
successful;* lit. *keep themselves most
upright*
σκοπεῖτε...ἐνθυμεῖσθε: both are
pres. imper.
καὶ μεταστάντων ἡμῶν: *also after
we retire (from the meeting);* aor. ppl.
< μεθίστημι in gen. abs.

17 **καὶ ἐνθυμεῖσθε...μὴ κατορθώσασαν:** *and ponder well and repeatedy
that you are taking counsel about the
city of your forebears, concerning (the
survival of) which single (city) (i.e. the
only one you have), the matter will
come down, in fact, to a single decision, for good or ill.* This sentence
has been called the most difficult in
Thuc. The difficulty may be due in
part to textual problems.
**τυχοῦσάν τε καὶ μὴ κατορθώσ-
ασαν:** the ppls. most likely modify
βουλήν, not an implied πόλιν; however, if their counsel succeeds, the city
will also survive, and if their counsel
fails, the city will be destroyed.

ἀμφότερος, -α, -ον: each of two, both
ἀνα-χωρέω: to go back, withdraw
ἀντι-λέγω: to speak in reply or against
ἀπο-κρίνομαι: to answer, reply
ἀφ-αιρέω (aor. -εῖλον): to take away from, remove
δή: indeed, surely, really, certainly, just
δοκέω: to seem, seem good, think, imagine
ἐλευθερία, ἡ: freedom, liberty
ἐπιτήδειος, -η, -ον: suitable; (of provisions) necessary
ἑπτακόσιοι, -αι, -α: seven hundred
ἔτος, -εως, τό: a year
θεῖος, -α, -ον: divine, sent by the gods
μετα-χωρέω: to withdraw, change place
μέχρι: as far as; as long as, until
μηδ-έτερος, -η, -ον: neither of the two
ὅδε, ἥδε, τόδε: this
οἰκέω: to live, dwell
ὅσπερ, ἥπερ, ὅπερ: the very one who, which; ἅπερ: as, like
ὅστις, ἥτις, ὅ τι: who- which-, whatever
οὔ-τε: and not, neither...nor
παραπλήσιος, -α, -ον: resembling; nearly
πειράω: to attempt, endeavor, try
πιστεύω: to trust, believe in, rely on
πολέμιος, -α, -ον: hostile, of the enemy
προ-καλέω: to call forth; propose or offer; (mostly mid.) provoke,
    challenge
σπονδή, ἡ: a drink-offering; truce, treaty
σφεῖς: they
σῴζω: to save, keep, preserve
τιμωρία, ἡ: punishment; help, aid
τύχη, ἡ: chance, luck, fortune, success
χρόνος, ὁ: time

Καὶ οἱ μὲν Ἀθηναῖοι μετεχώρησαν ἐκ τῶν λόγων· οἱ δὲ 112
Μήλιοι κατὰ σφᾶς αὐτοὺς γενόμενοι, ὡς ἔδοξεν αὐτοῖς
παραπλήσια καὶ ἀντέλεγον, ἀπεκρίναντο τάδε. ʽοὔτε ἄλλα
δοκεῖ ἡμῖν ἢ ἅπερ καὶ τὸ πρῶτον, ὦ Ἀθηναῖοι, οὔτ' ἐν
ὀλίγῳ χρόνῳ πόλεως ἑπτακόσια ἔτη ἤδη οἰκουμένης τὴν
ἐλευθερίαν ἀφαιρησόμεθα, ἀλλὰ τῇ τε μέχρι τοῦδε σῳζούσῃ 25
τύχῃ ἐκ τοῦ θείου αὐτὴν καὶ τῇ ἀπὸ τῶν ἀνθρώπων καὶ
Λακεδαιμονίων τιμωρίᾳ πιστεύοντες πειρασόμεθα σῴζεσθαι.
προκαλούμεθα δὲ ὑμᾶς φίλοι μὲν εἶναι, πολέμιοι δὲ μηδε-
τέροις, καὶ ἐκ τῆς γῆς ἡμῶν ἀναχωρῆσαι σπονδὰς ποιησαμένους αἵτινες δοκοῦσιν ἐπιτήδειοι εἶναι ἀμφοτέροις.'   30

---

21 **κατὰ σφᾶς αὐτοὺς γενόμενοι:** *once they were by themselves*
ὡς ἔδοξεν αὐτοῖς παραπλήσια καὶ ἀντέλεγον: *since their opinion was about the same as (what) they had been saying before in response (to the Athenians)*

22 **τάδε:** *as follows*
οὔτε ἄλλα δοκεῖ ἡμῖν ἤ: *neither does our opinion differ from*

23 **ἅπερ καὶ τὸ πρῶτον:** *what, in fact, (it was) initially*
ὦ Ἀθηναῖοι: the address marks a higher level of formality, perhaps a public pronouncement

24 **πόλεως...οἰκουμένης:** gen. w/ ἀφαιρησόμεθα
ἑπτακόσια ἔτη: acc. of extent of time; a "rhetorical number" indicating the city's longevity, not a specific foundation date

25 **τῇ...σῳζούσῃ τύχῃ:** *fortune, which has continued to preserve;* dat. w/ πιστεύοντες
μέχρι τοῦδε: *up to this (time)*

26 **ἐκ τοῦ θείου:** *divine*

αὐτὴν: *it;* i.e. the city, dir. obj. of σῳζούσῃ
τῇ...τιμωρίᾳ: *and on help;* another dat. w/ πιστεύοντες
ἀπὸ τῶν ἀνθρώπων: *from men;* i.e. vs. from the gods
καὶ Λακεδαιμονίων: *even from the Lacedaemonians;* perhaps a jab at the Aths.' earlier characterization of the Spartans

27 **προκαλούμεθα ὑμᾶς...ἀναχωρῆσαι:** *we propose that you... withdraw*

28 **φίλοι...μηδετέροις:** *(and that) we be (your) friends, while enemies to neither (side);* φίλοι and πολέμιοι are in nom. b/c they refer to the subj. of προκαλούμεθα

29 **σπονδὰς ποιησαμένους:** *after making a treaty;* ppl. agrees with an implied ἡμᾶς since both sides would swear oaths to a treaty

30 **αἵτινες δοκοῦσιν ἐπιτήδειοι εἶναι ἀμφοτέροις:** *which seems mutually agreeable;* αἵτινες is indef., lit. *whatever*

ἀπο-κρίνομαι: to answer, reply

ἀ-φανής, ές: unseen, unnoticed

βούλευμα, -ατος τό: deliberation, resolution

δή: indeed, surely, really, certainly, just

δια-λύω: to break apart, dissolve

δοκέω: to seem, seem good, think, imagine

θεάομαι: to see, watch, look at; consider

κρίνω: to choose, decide; interpret

μέλλω: to be about to, intend to

μόνος, -η, -ον: alone, only, solitary

οὖν: and so, then; so then; at any event

παρα-βάλλω: to cast (to one side), compare

πιστεύω: to trust, believe in, rely on

πλεῖστος, -η, -ον: most, very many

σαφής, -ές: clear, distinct, definite

σφάλλω: to make fall, overthrow, defeat; frustrate; (pass.) be overthrown;
    go wrong, be frustrated, be mistaken in something (gen.)

τοσοῦτος, -αύτη, -οῦτο: so (or such) great, so many, so much

τύχη, ἡ: chance, luck, fortune, success

Οἱ μὲν δὴ Μήλιοι τοσαῦτα ἀπεκρίναντο· οἱ δὲ Ἀθηναῖοι 113
διαλυόμενοι ἤδη ἐκ τῶν λόγων ἔφασαν, 'ἀλλ' οὖν μόνοι γε 1
ἀπὸ τούτων τῶν βουλευμάτων, ὡς ἡμῖν δοκεῖτε, τὰ μὲν
μέλλοντα τῶν ὁρωμένων σαφέστερα κρίνετε, τὰ δὲ ἀφανῆ
τῷ βούλεσθαι ὡς γιγνόμενα ἤδη θεᾶσθε, καὶ Λακεδαιμονίοις
καὶ τύχῃ καὶ ἐλπίσι πλεῖστον δὴ παραβεβλημένοι καὶ 5
πιστεύσαντες πλεῖστον καὶ σφαλήσεσθε.'

---

1 **διαλυόμενοι ἤδη ἐκ τῶν λόγων:** *breaking off from the exchange then*
ἀλλ' οὖν: *Well then;* another expression of exasperation
μόνοι γε: *you alone (of all men);* γε is emphatic

2 **ἀπὸ τούτων τῶν βουλευμάτων:** *to judge by these results of your deliberations*
τὰ μὲν μέλλοντα: *the future*

3 **τῶν ὁρωμένων:** *than what is before your eyes* (lit. *things that are seen*); gen. of comp. w/ σαφέστερα
τὰ δὲ ἀφανῆ…ὡς γιγνόμενα ἤδη θεᾶσθε: *as for the unseen (future), you view (it) as if it is already taking place;* γιγνόμενα, n. acc. pl. ppl. agreeing with τὰ ἀφανῆ, dir. obj. of θεᾶσθε

4 **τῷ βούλεσθαι:** *because you wish (it so);* causal dat.; or *by wishing (it so),* dat. of means
καὶ Λακεδαιμονίοις καὶ τύχῃ καὶ ἐλπίσι: construe all three datives w/ both παραβεβλημένοι and πιστεύσαντες

5 **πλεῖστον δὴ παραβεβλημένοι:** *indeed having given yourselves completely over to* or *having risked the most on;* pf. mid. ppl < παραβάλλω

6 **καὶ πιστεύσαντες πλεῖστον:** *and having put your utmost trust in*
καὶ σφαλήσεσθε: *you will also be (utterly) disappointed;* fut. ind. pass.; the Aths. implicitly warn that not just their expectations, but the Mels. themselves will be ruined.

ἀνα-χωρέω: to go back, withdraw
δι-αιρέω (aor. -εῖλον): to divide, distinguish
εὐθύς: right away, straight, directly, at once
κατα-λείπω: to leave behind, abandon
κύκλος, ὁ: a circle, round, ring
οὐδ-είς, οὐδε-μία, οὐδ-έν: no one, nothing
οὖν: and so, then; so then; at all events
παρα-μένω: to abide, remain, stay, stand fast,
περι-τειχίζω: to make a wall around
πλέων, -ον: more, greater
πολιορκέω: to beseige, form a blockade
πρέσβυς, -εως, ὁ: old, old (man), ambassador, envoy
σαφής, -ές: clear, distinct, definite
στράτευμα, τό: an expedition, campaign, army
στρατηγός, ὁ: general
σφεῖς: they
ὑπ-ακούω: to heed, listen to (gen.); to yield, submit, comply (dat.)
ὕστερος, -α, -ον: later, last
φυλακή, ἡ: guard, a watch, garrison
χωρίον, τό: place, spot, region

Καὶ οἱ μὲν Ἀθηναίων πρέσβεις ἀνεχώρησαν ἐς τὸ στρά- 114
τευμα· οἱ δὲ στρατηγοὶ αὐτῶν, ὡς οὐδὲν ὑπήκουον οἱ Μήλιοι,
πρὸς πόλεμον εὐθὺς ἐτρέποντο καὶ διελόμενοι κατὰ πόλεις περιετείχισαν κύκλῳ τοὺς Μηλίους. καὶ ὕστερον φυλακὴν σφῶν 10
τε αὐτῶν καὶ τῶν ξυμμάχων καταλιπόντες οἱ Ἀθηναῖοι καὶ
κατὰ γῆν καὶ κατὰ θάλασσαν ἀνεχώρησαν τῷ πλέονι τοῦ στρα-
τοῦ. οἱ δὲ λειπόμενοι παραμένοντες ἐπολιόρκουν τὸ χωρίον.

---

8 **οἱ δὲ στρατηγοὶ αὐτῶν:** *their generals;* i.e. the commanders of the Athenian forces as opposed to the πρέσβεις, the Ath. delegation to Melos
ὡς: *when* or *since*
οὐδὲν ὑπήκουον οἱ Μήλιοι: *the Melians were not yielding* (or *submitting*) *at all*

9 **πρὸς πόλεμον εὐθὺς ἐτρέποντο:** *immediately they turned to war;* i.e. commenced hostilities; imperf. b/c the action was ongoing
διελόμενοι κατὰ πόλεις: *once they divided (their troops) by cities;* i.e. into contingents by city; διελόμενοι, aor. mid. ppl. < διαιρέω

περιετείχισαν κύκλῳ τοὺς Μηλίους: *they encircled the Melians with a wall* (lit. *walled them round in a circle*)

10 **φυλακὴν σφῶν τε αὐτῶν καὶ τῶν ξυμμάχων:** *a garrison (comprised of) their own men and their allies;* including ships and crews

11 **καὶ κατὰ γῆν καὶ κατὰ θάλασσαν:** *by both land and sea*
τῷ πλέονι: *with the majority;* dat. of accompaniment

13 **οἱ δὲ λειπόμενοι:** *the remainder (of the forces)*

Ἀργεῖος, -α, -ον: Argive, of Argos

ἀφ-ίημι: to send forth, let go free; give up

διά: through (gen.); on account of (acc.)

δια-φθείρω: to destroy utterly, disable

ἐσ-βάλλω: to cast onto, put on board; invade

ἴδιος, -α, -ον: one's own, peculiar

κηρύσσω: to proclaim, be a herald

Κορίνθιος, -η, -ον: Corinthian

λεία, ἡ: loot, plunder

ληΐζομαι: to seize as loot, plunder

λοχίζω: to place as an ambush; (pass.) to be ambushed

ὀγδοήκοντα: eighty

οὐ-δέ: and not, but not, nor, not even

παρά: from, from the side of (gen.); beside, alongside (dat.); to the side of; past, beyond; compared to (acc.)

πολεμέω: to wage war, go to war, make war upon; fight, do battle with

Πύλος, -ου, ἡ: Pylos, a city in the Peloponnese

σπονδή, ἡ: a drink-offering; truce, treaty

σφεῖς: they

σφέτερος, -η, -ον: their own, their

ὑπό: (gen.) by, because of, from; (dat.) under

Φλειάσιος, -α, -ον: Phleiasian (Phleia was a city near Argos)

φυγάς, -άδος, ὁ: fugitive, an exile

Καὶ Ἀργεῖοι κατὰ τὸν χρόνον τὸν αὐτὸν ἐσβαλόντες ἐς   115
τὴν Φλειασίαν καὶ λοχισθέντες ὑπό τε Φλειασίων καὶ τῶν   15
σφετέρων φυγάδων διεφθάρησαν ὡς ὀγδοήκοντα. καὶ οἱ ἐκ
τῆς Πύλου Ἀθηναῖοι Λακεδαιμονίων πολλὴν λείαν ἔλαβον·
καὶ Λακεδαιμόνιοι δι' αὐτὸ τὰς μὲν σπονδὰς οὐδ' ὣς ἀφέντες
ἐπολέμουν αὐτοῖς, ἐκήρυξαν δὲ εἴ τις βούλεται παρὰ σφῶν
Ἀθηναίους λῄζεσθαι. καὶ Κορίνθιοι ἐπολέμησαν ἰδίων τινῶν   20

---

14 Καὶ Ἀργεῖοι: The scene shifts back to the mainland, where hostilities heighten, but the Peace of Nicias still holds, at least nominally. The Argives here are of the democratic faction favoring Athens.

κατὰ τὸν χρόνον τὸν αὐτὸν: *at the same time;* = κατὰ τὸν αὐτὸν χρόνον

ἐς τὴν Φλειασίαν: supply γῆν; Phleia (N. E. of Argos) is where the exiled Argive oligarchs were residing.

καὶ τῶν σφετέρων φυγάδων: *and by their own* (i.e. Argive) *exiles*

16 διεφθάρησαν: 3p. aor. pass. < διαφθείρω

ὡς ὀγδοήκοντα: *about 80;* subj. of διεφθάρησαν

καὶ οἱ ἐκ τῆς Πύλου Ἀθηναῖοι: "the Athenians from Pylos" means "the Athenians and their troops from Pylos" since most were probably Messenians and former helots (Spartan slaves). In 424, after the Spartans on the island of Sphacteria (in the harbor of Pylos, on the S.W. coast of the Peloponnese) surrendered, the Aths. garrisoned the town, settled former helots there, and refused to give it up in accordance with Peace of Nicias.

17 Λακεδαιμονίων: *from,* or *belonging to the Lacedaemonians*

18 δι' αὐτὸ: *wherefore;* b/c of the raiding and pillaging

τὰς μὲν σπονδὰς οὐδ' ὣς ἀφέντες ἐπολέμουν αὐτοῖς: *although not even so did they abandon the peace and go to war with them* [the Aths.]; ἀφέντες, aor. ppl. < ἀφίημι

19 ἐκήρυξαν δὲ εἴ τις βούλεται παρὰ σφῶν Ἀθηναίους λῄζεσθαι: *they proclaimed by herald that if anyone on their side wanted to plunder the Athenians;* supply something like *he should do so* or *let him do so.* Thuc. retains the original tense of the proclamation calling for volunteers: εἴ τις βούλεται.

20 ἰδίων τινῶν [διαφορῶν ἕνεκα]: *because of some differences of their own;* i.e. differences the Corinthians did not share with the Spartans or the alliance as a whole. About these differences Thuc. is silent.

ἀγορά, ἡ: agora, marketplace

αἱρέω: to seize, take, (aor. εἷλον); (mid.) choose

ἀμείνων, ἄμεινον: better

ἀνα-χωρέω: to go back, withdraw

ἀπο-κτείνω: to kill, slay

Ἀργεῖος, -α, -ον: Argive, of Argos

δια-βατήρια, ἡ: an offering before crossing

δια-φορά, ἡ: difference; quarrel

δύναμαι: to be able, can, be capable

ἕνεκα: for the sake of, because of (gen.)

ἔπ-ειτα: then, next, secondly

ἐπι-γίγνομαι: to come after or next, to follow (upon); to befall

ἐσ-φέρω: to introduce, propose, carry in

ἡσυχάζω: to keep quiet, rest (from war)

θέρος, τό: summer

ἱερός, -ά, -όν: holy; sacrificial victim; temple

μέλλω: to be about to, intend to

νύξ, νυκτός, ἡ: night

ὅριον, τό: boundary, limit

παρασκευάζω: to prepare, get ready

Πελοποννήσιος, -α, -ον: Peloponnessian

περι-τείχισμα, τό: encircling wall

πλεῖστος, -η, -ον: most, very many

προσ-βάλλω: to attack, strike against, dash

σῖτος, ὁ: grain, bread, food

στρατεύω: to march, campaign

τελευτάω: to end, complete, finish; die

φυλακή, ἡ: a guard, watch, garrison

χειμών, -ῶνος τό: storm, winter

χρήσιμος, -η, -ον: good, useful, serviceable

διαφορῶν ἕνεκα τοῖς Ἀθηναίοις· οἱ δ' ἄλλοι Πελοποννήσιοι
ἡσύχαζον. εἷλον δὲ καὶ οἱ Μήλιοι τῶν Ἀθηναίων τοῦ
περιτειχίσματος τὸ κατὰ τὴν ἀγορὰν προσβαλόντες νυκτός,
καὶ ἄνδρας τε ἀπέκτειναν καὶ ἐσενεγκάμενοι σῖτόν τε καὶ
ὅσα πλεῖστα ἐδύναντο χρήσιμα ἀναχωρήσαντες ἡσύχαζον· 25
καὶ οἱ Ἀθηναῖοι ἄμεινον τὴν φυλακὴν τὸ ἔπειτα παρεσκευά-
ζοντο. καὶ τὸ θέρος ἐτελεύτα.

Τοῦ δ' ἐπιγιγνομένου χειμῶνος Λακεδαιμόνιοι μελλή- 116
σαντες ἐς τὴν Ἀργείαν στρατεύειν, ὡς αὐτοῖς τὰ διαβατήρια
[ἱερὰ ἐν τοῖς ὁρίοις] οὐκ ἐγίγνετο, ἀνεχώρησαν. καὶ Ἀρ- 30

---

21 **τοῖς Ἀθηναίοις:** dat. w / διαφορῶν
οἱ δ' ἄλλοι Πελοποννήσιοι: *the rest
of the Peloponnesians*

22 **εἷλον:** aor. indic. act. 3p < αἱρέω
τοῦ περιτειχίσματος: *of the siege
wall;* part. gen. w/ τὸ κατὰ τὴν
ἀγορὰν
τὸ κατὰ τὴν ἀγορὰν: *the part
along* (i.e. opposite) *the (Melians')
marketplace*

23 **νυκτός:** gen. of time during which

24 **ἐσενεγκάμενοι:** aor. ppl. mid.
< ἐσφέφω

25 **ὅσα πλεῖστα ἐδύναντο χρήσιμα:**
as many supplies as they could

26 **ἄμεινον τὴν φυλακὴν...παρε-
σκευάζοντο:** *(the Athenians)
improved their watch*
τὸ ἔπειτα: *then;* the article does not
affect the sense.

28 **μελλήσαντες:** *were about to;* i.e.
intended to; aor. ppl. < μέλλω; here
the verb does not refer to delay, as is
clear from the Argives' reaction.

29 **ὡς τὰ διαβατήρια...οὐκ ἐγίγνετο:**
*when the border sacrifices were not
(favorable);* the bracketed words ἱερὰ
ἐν τοῖς ὁρίοις are unnecessary; most
likely they are an explanation of
διαβατήρια and were introduced into
the text from the margin of a
manuscript.

Thucydides

Ἀθῆναι, αἱ: Athens
αἱρέω: to seize, take, (aor. εἷλον); (mid.) choose
ἀνδρα-ποδίζω: to reduce to slavery, enslave
ἄπ-οικος, ὁ: colonist, settler
ἀπο-κτείνω: to kill, slay
αὖθις: back, back again, backwards
βουλεύω: to deliberate, plan, take counsel
Δημέας, -ου, ὁ: Demeas
διά: through (gen.); on account of (acc.)
δια-φεύγω: to flee, get away from, escape
ἑαυτοῦ (αὑτοῦ) -ῆς, -οῦ: him-, her-, itself
ἐκεῖνος, -η, -ον: that, those
ἕτερος, -α, -ον: one of two, other, different
ἡβάω: to be in the prime of youth, young; in the prime of life
κράτος, -εος, τό: strength, power
μέλλησις, ἡ: intention; delay
ξυγ-χωρέω: to come together, agree, assent
ξυλ-λαμβάνω: to help; collect, gather
οἰκίζω: to settle, colonize, people
πάρ-ειμι: to be near, be present, be at hand; (impersonal) to be in one's power
πεντακόσιοι, -αι, -α: five hundred
περι-τείχισμα, τό: encircling wall
πολιορκέω: to beseige, form a blockade
προ-δοσία, ἡ: betrayal, treason, giving up
στρατία, ἡ: an army, expedition, land force
ὑπ-οπτεύω: to suspect, hold in suspicion
ὕστερος, -α, -ον: later, last
Φιλοκράτης, ὁ: Philocrates; nothing else is known about this commander
φυλακή, ἡ: guard, a watch, garrison
χωρίον, τό: place, spot, region
ὥστε: so that, that, so as to, and so

γεῖοι διὰ τὴν ἐκείνων μέλλησιν τῶν ἐν τῇ πόλει τινὰς ὑπο-
πτεύσαντες τοὺς μὲν ξυνέλαβον, οἱ δ' αὐτοὺς καὶ διέφυγον.
καὶ οἱ Μήλιοι περὶ τοὺς αὐτοὺς χρόνους αὖθις καθ' ἕτερόν
τι τοῦ περιτειχίσματος εἷλον τῶν Ἀθηναίων, παρόντων οὐ
πολλῶν τῶν φυλάκων. καὶ ἐλθούσης στρατιᾶς ὕστερον ἐκ   5
τῶν Ἀθηνῶν ἄλλης, ὡς ταῦτα ἐγίγνετο, ἧς ἦρχε Φιλοκράτης
ὁ Δημέου, καὶ κατὰ κράτος ἤδη πολιορκούμενοι, γενομένης
καὶ προδοσίας τινός ἀφ' ἑαυτῶν, ξυνεχώρησαν τοῖς Ἀθηναίοις
ὥστε ἐκείνους περὶ αὐτῶν βουλεῦσαι. οἱ δὲ ἀπέκτειναν
Μηλίων ὅσους ἡβῶντας ἔλαβον, παῖδας δὲ καὶ γυναῖκας   10
ἠνδραπόδισαν· τὸ δὲ χωρίον αὐτοὶ ᾤκισαν, ἀποίκους ὕστερον
πεντακοσίους πέμψαντες.

---

1 **διὰ τὴν ἐκείνων μέλλησιν**: *because of their* (i.e. the Spartans') *intention*; i.e. the preparations that indicated their intentions
τῶν ἐν τῇ πόλει τινὰς ὑποπτεύσ-αντες: *suspicious of some men in the city*; i.e. those of oligarchical (pro-Spartan) leanings

2 **τοὺς μὲν...οἱ δ'**: *some...others*
αὐτοὺς: *them*; i.e. the Argive democrats pursuing the pro-Spartan faction

3 **περὶ τοὺς αὐτοὺς χρόνους**: *around the same time*
αὖθις καθ' ἕτερόν τι τοῦ περι-τειχίσματος: *again took a part of the siege wall, (but) in another area*

4 **παρόντων...φυλάκων**: gen. abs

5 **ἐλθούσης στρατιᾶς...ἄλλης**: gen. abs.

6 **ὡς ταῦτα ἐγίγνετο**: *since this was the situation*

7 **καὶ κατὰ κράτος ἤδη πολιορκού-μενοι**: *and under very tight siege then*; i.e. a siege conducted with all their might, κατὰ κράτος
γενομένης καὶ προδοσίας τινός ἀφ' ἑαυτῶν: *there also having been a betrayal from within* (lit. *from their own men*); gen. abs.

8 **ξυνεχώρησαν τοῖς Ἀθηναίοις ὥστε ἐκείνους περὶ αὐτῶν βουλεῦσαι**: *they came to terms with the Athenians (with the understanding) that they* (i.e. the Aths. in Athens) *deliberate about them* (i.e. the Mels.)

10 **Μηλίων ὅσους ἡβῶντας**: *however many Melians were in their prime*; presumably this comprised all men of fighting age who surrendered or were caught by the Athenians.

11 **αὐτοὶ ᾤκισαν**: *they themselves settled*; aor. < οἰκίζω

Vocabulary

A

ἀγαθός, ή, όν: good, brave, capable

ἀγορά, ἡ: agora, marketplace

ἄγω: to lead, bring, carry, convey

ἀγωγή, ἡ: a bringing, carrying away

ἀγών, ὁ: contest, trial

ἀγωνίζομαι: to contend, compete, fight

ἀ-δικέω: to be unjust, do wrong, injure

Ἀθῆναι, αἱ: Athens

Ἀθηναῖος, α, ον: Athenian, of Athens

ἀ-θυμέω: to be disheartened, lose hope
for; fear greatly

αἰεί: always, forever, in every case

αἵρεσις, εως, ὁ: choice

αἱρέω: to seize, take, (aor. εἷλον); (mid.)
choose

αἰσχρός, ά, όν: shameful, disgraceful

αἰσχύνη, ἡ: shame, disgrace, dishonor

ἀκούω: to hear, listen to

ἀκριβής, ές: accurate, precise, exact

ἄκων (ἀέκων), ἄκουσα, ἄκον:
unwilling

ἀληθής, ές: true

Ἀλκιβιάδης, ὁ: Alcibiades

ἀλλά: but

ἀλλήλος, α, ον: one another

ἄλλος, η, ο: other, one...another

ἄλλως: otherwise, in another way; in
vain

ἀ-λογία, ἡ: want of reason, absurdity.
rashness

ἀ-λόγιστος, ον: unreasonable,
thoughtless; reckless, rash

ἄ-λογος, ον: without speech contrary to
reason

ἅμα: at the same time; along with (dat.)

ἀμείνων, ἄμεινον: better

ἀμφότερος, α, ον: each of two, both

ἄν: (a modal particle)

ἀναγκάζω: to force, compel, require

ἀναγκαῖος, α, ον: necessary, inevitable

ἀνάγκη, ἡ: necessity, force, constraint

ἀν-αρκτος, ον: not governed,
ungoverned

ἀνα-ρρίπτω: to toss up (dice); run a risk

ἀναχωρέω: to go back, withdraw

ἀνδρ-αγαθία, ἡ: bravery, manly virtue

ἀνδρα-ποδίζω: to reduce to slavery,
enslave

ἀν-έλεγκτος, ον: not to be questioned

ἀν-έλπιστος, ον: hopeless, having no
hope

ἀν-επιστήμων, ον: unskilled, ignorant

ἀν-ήκεστος, ον: incurable, irreparable,
fatal

ἀνήρ, ἀνδρός, ὁ: man, husband

ἀνθ-ίστημι: to set against; stand against

ἀνθρώπειος, α, ον: human

ἄνθρωπος, ὁ: human being

ἄ-νοια, ἡ: folly, a lack of understanding

ἀντί: in place of; for the sake of (gen.)

ἀντι-λέγω: to speak in reply or against

ἀντι-τάσσω: to arrange against, set
opposite

ἀξιόω: to deem or think worthy

ἀπ-αλλάσσω: to set free, release from;
end, leave off, cease from; (mid.)
depart

ἅπας, ἅπασα, ἅπαν: every, quite all

ἀπατάω: to cheat, trick, deceive, beguile

ἀ-πειρόκακος, ον: without experience
of evil, ignorant of evil

ἀ-πιστία, ἡ: disbelief, distrust, mistrust

ἄ-πιστος, ον: not trustworthy, unreliable; not trusting

ἀπό: from, away from (gen.)

ἄποικος, ὁ: colonist, settler

ἀπο-κρίνομαι: to answer, reply

ἀπο-κτείνω: to kill, slay

ἄ-πονος, ον: without toil, untroubled

ἄ-πορος, ον: difficult, impracticable

ἀπο-χωρέω: to go from, depart, withdraw

ἀ-πρεπής, ές: unseemly, improper

ἄρα: then, therefore, it seems, it turns out

Ἀργεῖος, α, ον: Argive, of Argos

Ἄργος, τό: Argos

ἀρέσκω: to please, satisfy, appease

ἀρετή, ἡ: excellence, goodness, virtue

ἀρχή, ἡ: a beginning; rule, office

ἄρχω: to begin; rule, be leader of

ἀ-σθένεια, ἡ: weakness, feebleness

ἀ-σθενής, ές: weak, feeble, sick

ἀ-σφάλεια, ἡ: security, assurance

ἀ-σφαλής, ές: safe, secure, trusty, not liable to move or fall

αὖ: again, once more; further, moreover

αὖθις: back, back again, backwards

αὐτός, ή, ό: self; he, she, it; the same

ἀφ-αιρέω: to take away from, remove

ἀ-φανής, ές: unseen, unnoticed

ἀφ-ίημι: to send forth, let go free; give up

ἀφ-ίστημι: to revolt; withdraw, stand afar

ἄ-φρων, ον: senseless, foolish, silly

B

βέβαιος, α, ον: steadfast, steady, firm

βλάπτω: to harm, hurt, damage

βλέπω: to look at, see

βοηθέω: to come to aid, assist, aid

βούλευμα, ατος τό: deliberation, resolution

βουλεύω: to deliberate, plan, take counsel

βουλή, ἡ: council, plan, will

βούλησις, εως, ἡ: wish, will; purpose

βούλομαι: to wish, be willing, desire

Βρασίδας, ὁ: Brasidas

βραχύς, έα, ύ: short

Γ

γάρ: for, since

γε: at least, at any rate; indeed

γῆ, ἡ: earth

γίγνομαι: to come to be, become, be born

γιγνώσκω: to come to know, learn, recognize; to form a judgement, think

γνώμη, ἡ: judgment, resolve, opinion

γνωρίζω: to make known, gain knowledge of

γοῦν: γε οὖν, at least, at any rate, any way

γυνή, γυναικός, ἡ: a woman, wife

Δ

δάπανος, ον: extravagant, lavish

δέ: but, and, on the other hand

δεῖ: it is necessary, must, ought (+ inf.)

δειλία, ἡ: cowardice

δεινός, ή, όν: terrible; wondrous, clever

δέχομαι: to receive, accept

δή: indeed, surely, really, certainly, just

δηιόω: to slay, cut down; waste, ravage

δηλόω: to make clear, show, reveal

Δήμεος, ου, ὁ: Demeas

διά: through (gen.); on account of (acc.)

δια-βατήρια, ἡ: an offering before
    crossing
δι-αιρέω: to divide, distinguish
διακόσιοι, αι, α: two hundred
δια-λύω: to break apart, dissolve
δια-μέλλησις, εως ἡ: postponement;
    intention
διάνοια, ἡ: thought, intention, purpose
δια-πράσσω: to accomplish, effect
δια-φέρω: to carry over; differ, disagree
δια-φεύγω: to flee, get away from, escape
δια-φθείρω: to destroy utterly, disable
δια-φορά, ἡ: difference; quarrel
διδάσκω: to teach, instruct
δίδωμι: to give
δίκαιος, α, ον: just, right, lawful, fair
δικαιόω: to deem right, think right
δικαίωμα, τό: plea of right, justification,
    act setting a wrong right
δοκέω: to seem, seem good, think,
    imagine
δόξα, ἡ: expectation, reputation, opinion
δουλεία, ἡ: servitude, slavery, bondage
δουλεύω: to be a slave, serve, be subject
    to
δράω: to do, act
δύναμαι: to be able, can, be capable
δύναμις, εως, ἡ: power, force, capacity
δυνατός, ή, όν: capable, strong, possible
δύο: two

E

ἐάν (εἰ ἄν): if
ἑαυτοῦ (αὑτοῦ), ῆς, οῦ: him-, her-,
    itself
ἐγγύς: near (gen.); adv. nearby
ἐγχειρίζω: to entrust; take in hand
ἐθέλω: to be willing, wish, desire

εἰ: if, whether
εἶδον: saw, beheld (aor. of ὁράω)
εἰκός, ότος, τό: likelihood, what is
    likely, probable, reasonable (neut. pf.
    ppl. < ἔοικα)
εἴκοσι: twenty
εἴκω: to yield, give way, retire
εἰμί: to be, exist
εἶπον: (aor.) said, spoke
εἰς (ἐς): into, to, in regard to (acc.)
εἷς, μία, ἕν: one, single, alone
ἐκ, ἐξ: out of, from (gen.)
ἕκαστος, η, ον: each, every one
ἑκάτερος, α, ον: each of two, either
ἐκ-βιβάζω: to make go out, cause to go
    out; to stop one from
ἐκεῖνος, η, ον: that, those
ἑκών, ἑκοῦσα, ἑκόν: willing,
    intentionally
ἐλασσόω: to lessen; (pass.) to suffer loss,
    be inferior, be at a disadvantage
ἐλευθερία, ἡ: freedom, liberty
ἐλεύθερος, η, ον: free
ἐλλείπω: to fall short, lack; leave behind
Ἕλλην, Ἕλληνος, ὁ: a Greek
ἐλπίζω: to hope for, look for, expect
ἐλπίς, ίδος, ἡ: hope, expectation
ἐν: in, on, among (dat.)
ἐνδίδωμαι: to give in, surrender; allow
ἕνεκα: for the sake of, because of (gen.)
ἐνθυμέομαι: to take to he art, consider,
    ponder
ἐνταῦθα: here, hither, there, thither,
    then
ἐντός: within, inside
ἕξ: six
ἔξω: out of (gen.); adv. outside

ἐπάγω: to bring to or against; urge

ἐπαγωγός, όν: attractive, luring on, alluring

ἐπειδάν: whenever

ἐπειδή: when, after, since, because

ἔπειτα: then, next, secondly

ἐπ-εξ-έρχομαι: to go out against, proceed against; go through

ἐπ-έρχομαι: to come upon; attack

ἐπί: near, at (gen.), to (acc), upon (dat.)

ἐπι-γίγνομαι: to come after or next, to follow (upon); to befall

ἐπι-είκεια, ἡ: reasonableness; equity

ἐπι-καλέω: to call upon, summon

ἐπι-λείπω: to leave behind; fail, be wanting

ἐπι-σπάω: to bring on; draw to, entice; persuade

ἐπίσταμαι: to know

ἐπιτήδειος, η, ον: suitable; (of provisions) necessary

ἐπι-τίθημι: to put upon; add; set upon, attack

ἐπι-τρέπω: to turn toward; turn over to, entrust to; rely on

ἐπι-φανής, ές: manifest, evident

ἐπι-χώριος, α, ον: local, native

ἑπτακόσιοι, αι, α: seven hundred

ἔργον, τό: work, labor, deed, act

ἐρέω: will speak (fut. of λέγω)

ἔρχομαι, εἶμι, ἦλθον: to come or go

ἐσ-άπαξ: at once, once of all

ἐσ-βάλλω: to cast onto, put on board; invade

ἐσ-φέρω: to introduce, propose, carry in

ἕτερος, α, ον: one of two, other, different

ἔτι: still, besides, further

ἔτος, εως, τό: a year

εὖ: well

εὐθύς: right away, straight, directly, at once

εὐ-μένεια, ἡ: favor, goodwill

εὔ-νους, ουν: well disposed to, kind to

ἔχθρα, ἡ: hatred

ἐχυρός, ά, όν: strong, secure

ἔχω: to have, hold; be able; be disposed

Z–H

ζηλόω: to envy, be jealous; vie with

ἤ: or (either…or); than

ἦ: truly, in truth

ἡβάω: to be in the prime of youth, young; in the prime of life

ἡγέομαι: to lead; consider, think, believe

ἤδη: already, now, at this time

ἡδύς, εῖα, ύ: pleasant; pleasing

ἤκιστος, η, ον: least; not at all

ἥκω: to have come, be present

ἡμεῖς: we

ἡμέτερος, α, ον: our, ours

ἤν (ἐάν, εἰ ἄν): if, if ever

ἠπειρώτης, ὁ: mainlander

ἡσσάομαι: to be less or weaker than, inferior to; to be defeated

ἥσσων, ον: less, weaker, inferior

ἡσυχάζω: to keep quiet, rest (from war)

ἡσυχία, ἡ: silence, quiet, stillness, rest, leisure

Θ

θάλασσα, ἡ: sea

θεάομαι: to see, watch, look at; consider

θεῖος, α, ον: divine, sent by the gods

θέρος, τό: summer

θρασύνω: to embolden, encourage

I

ἴδιος, α, ον: one's own, peculiar

ἱερός, ά, όν: holy; sacrificial victim;
  temple

ἱππο-τοξότης, ὁ: horsemounted archer

ἴσος, η, ον: equal to, the same as, like

ἵστημι: to make stand, set up, stop,
  establish

ἰσχυρός, ά, όν: strong, powerful

K

καθ-αιρέω: to take down (by force),
  destroy

κάθ-ημαι: to sit

καθ-ίστημι: to set up, establish; to
  · become, bring into a certain state

καί: and, also, even, too

καίτοι: and yet, and indeed, and further

κακότης, ητος, ἡ: baseness cowardice

καλέω: to call, summon, invite

καλός, ή, όν: beautiful, fair, noble, fine

καλῶς: well, beautifully

κατά: down from (gen.), down (acc.)

κατα-λείπω: to leave behind, abandon

κατα-λύω: to put down, destroy

κατα-στρέφω: to upset, overturn; (mid.)
  subdue

κατα-τίθημι: to put down, deposit, settle

κατ-ορθόω: to set upright, erect

κεῖμαι: to lie, lie down; to be laid down,
  established (as in laws)

κελεύω: to bid, order, command, exhort

κερδαίνω: to gain, make a profit

κηρύσσω: to proclaim, be a herald

κινδινεύω: to risk, venture; to be
  probable

κίνδυνος, ὁ: risk, danger, venture

Κλεομήδης, ὁ: Cleomedes

κοινός, ή, όν: common, ordinary; public

Κορίνθιος, η, ον: Corinthian

κρατέω: to be strong; conquer, prevail

κράτος, εος, τό: strength, power

κρείσσων, ον: better, stronger, superior

Κρητικός, η, ον: from Crete, Cretan

κρίνω: to choose, decide; interpret

κριτής, οῦ, ὁ: judge, decider

κύκλος, ὁ: a circle, round, ring

Λ

Λακεδαιμόνιος, α, ον: Lacedaemonian

λαμβάνω: to take, receive, catch, grasp

λανθάνω: to escape notice of, act unnoticed

λέγω: to say, speak

λεία, ἡ: loot, plunder

λείπω: to leave, forsake, abandon

Λέσβιος, α, ον: Lesbian, of Lesbos

ληίζομαι: to seize as loot, plunder

λῆψις, εως, ἡ: seizure

λογίζομαι: to reckon, calculate, account

λόγος, ὁ: word, speech, discourse,
  argument

λοιπός, ή, όν: remaining, the rest

λοχίζω: to place as an ambush; (pass.) to
  be ambushed

Λυκομήδης, ους, ὁ: Lycomedes

λυμαίνομαι: to outrage, maltreat; cause
  ruin

M

μακαρίζω: to deem blessed or happy

μάλιστα: most of all; certainly,
  especially; (with numbers)
  approximately

μᾶλλον: more, rather

μαντικός, ή, όν: prophetic

μεγαλύνω: to make great, strengthen, exalt

μέγιστος, η, ον: greatest, best, longest

μεθ-ίστημι: to change (place); remove

μέλλησις, ἡ: intention; delay

μέλλω: to be about to, intend to

μέν: on the one hand

μέντοι: however, nevertheless; certainly

μετά: with (gen.); after (acc.)

μετα-χωρέω: to withdraw, change place

μέτριος, α, ον: moderate, temperate

μέχρι: as far as; as long as, until

μή: not, lest

μηδέ: and not, but not, nor

μηδ-έτερος, η, ον: neither of the two

Μῆδος, ὁ: a Mede; the Persians

μῆκος, τό: length

Μήλιος, α, ον: Melian, from Melos

Μῆλος, ὁ: Melos

μῖσος, εος, τό: hate, hatred

μόνος, η, ον: alone, only, solitary

N

ναυ-κράτωρ, ὁ, ἡ: master of the sea, (lit.) master of a ship

ναῦς, νεώς, ἡ: a ship, boat

νησιῶται, οἱ: islanders

νῆσος, ἡ: an island

νικάω: to conquer, defeat, win

νομίζω: to believe, think, deem

νόμιμος, η, ον: customary

νόμισις, εως, ἡ: belief, opinion

νόμος, ὁ: law, custom

νῦν: now; as it is

νύξ, νυκτός, ἡ: night

Ξ

ξυγ-γένεια, ἡ: kinship, family

ξυγ-γενής, ές: akin to, kindred; of like kind

ξυγ-γνώμη, ἡ: forgiveness, pardon

ξυγ-χωρέω: to come together, agree, assent

ξυλ-λαμβάνω: to help; collect, gather

ξυμ-βαίνω: to stand with; come to an agreement; to happen, turn out (in a certain way)

ξυμ-μαχέω: to fight along side, be an ally

ξυμ-μαχία, ἡ: an alliance

ξυμ-μαχίς, ίδος: allied (fem. of adj. ξύμμαχος)

ξύμ-μαχος, ον: allied, fighting along with

ξυμ-φέρω: to bring together; to come to terms, agree; (of events) to happen; to confer a benefit, be useful, be expedient

ξυμ-φορά, ἡ: misfortune, mishap, event

ξύμ-φορος, ον: advantageous, useful, expedient; (as subst.) interest, advantage

ξυν-αγωνίζομαι: to contend or fight alongside

ξυν-αιρέω: to grasp, take together

ξύν-εδρος, ὁ: commissioner, councilor

ξυν-εχής, ές: continuous

ξυν-ήκω: to have come together, meet

ξύν-οδος, ἡ: encounter, meeting

ξυ-στρατεύω: to compaign together

O

ὁ, ἡ, τό: the

ὀγδοήκοντα: eighty

ὅδε, ἥδε, τόδε: this

οἶδα: to know

οἰκεῖος, α, ον: intimate, close, related

οἰκέω: to live, dwell

οἰκίζω: to settle, colonize, people

οἴομαι: to suppose, think, imagine

οἷος, α, ον: of what sort, as

ὀλίγος η, ον: few, little, small

ὁμοιόω: to make like, assimilate; be like

ὅμως: nevertheless, however, yet

ὄνομα, τό: name, phrase, expression

ὁπλίτης, ου, ὁ: hoplite, armed soldier

ὅπως: how, in what way; in order that, that

ὁράω: to see, look, behold

ὀρθόω: to set straight, set upright

ὀρθῶς: correctly, straightly, rightly

ὅριον, τό: boundary, limit

ὅς, ἥ, ὅ: who, which, that

ὅσιος, α, ον: holy; pious, religious; righteous, lawful

ὅσος, η, ον: as much or as; all who

ὅσπερ, ἥπερ, ὅπερ: the very one who, which; ἅπερ: as, like

ὅστις, ἥτις, ὅ τι: who-, which-, whatever

ὅταν: ὅτε ἄν, whenever

ὅτε: when, at what time

ὅτι: that (see also ὅστις)

οὗ: where

οὐ, οὐκ, οὐχ: not

οὐ-δέ: and not, but not, nor, not even

οὐδ-είς, οὐδεμία, οὐδέν: no one, nothing

οὐδ-έτερος, η, ον: neither of the two

οὔ-κουν: certainly not, and so not

οὖν: and so, then; so then; at all events

οὔ-τε: and not; οὔτε…οὔτε: neither …nor

οὗτος, αὕτη, τοῦτο: this, these

οὕτως: in this way, thus, so

ὀφλισκάνω (aor. ὦφλον): to owe; be liable to pay a fine; be found guilty; to incur a charge of, bring upon oneself (acc.)

Π

παῖς, παιδός, ὁ, ἡ: a child, boy, girl; slave

παντ-άπασι: all in all, altogether, entirely

παρά: from, from the side of (gen.); beside, alongside (dat.); to the side of; past, beyond; compared to (acc.)

παρα-βάλλω: to cast (to one side), compare

παρά-δειγμα, τό: example, proof

παρα-κινδύνευσις, εως, ἡ: desperate venture

παρα-λαμβάνω: to receive, undertake, inherit

παρα-μένω: to abide, remain, stay, stand fast

παρα-μύθιον, τό: encouragement, exhortation; an abatement, assuagement, consolation

παραπλήσιος, α, ον: resembling; nearly

παρασκευάζω: to prepare, get ready

παρασκευή, ἡ: preparation; intrigue

πάρ-ειμι: to be near, be present, be at hand; (impersonal) to be in one's power

παρ-έχω: to provide, furnish, give

παρ-οξύνω: to urge on, provoke; irritate

πᾶς, πᾶσα, πᾶν: every, all, the whole

πάσχω: to suffer, experience

πατρίς, ίδος, ἡ: fatherland, land of one's forbears, native land

παύω: to stop, make cease

πείθω: to persuade, win over, trust; (mid.) obey

πειράω: to attempt, endeavor, try

πέλαγος, τό: sea

πέλας: near

Πελοπόννησος, ἡ: the Peloponnese

πέμπω: to send, conduct, convey, dispatch

πεντακόσιοι, αι, α: five hundred

περαιόω: to cross

περί: around, about, concerning (all cases)

περιγίγνομαι: to prevail over, be superior (to)

περιουσία, ἡ: surplus, abundance; advantage

περιπίπτω: to fall on, be wrecked

περιτειχίζω: to make a wall around

περιτείχισμα, τό: encircling wall

πιέζω: to press, weigh down, squeeze

πιστεύω: to trust, believe in, rely on

πιστός, ή, όν: trustworthy, loyal; credible

πλεῖστος, η, ον: most, very many

πλέω: to sail

πλέων, ον: more, greater

πλῆθος, τό: crowd, multitude; size

ποιέω: to do, make, create; (mid.) consider

πολεμέω: to wage war, go to war, make war upon; fight, do battle with

πολέμιος, α, ον: hostile, of the enemy

πόλεμος, ὁ: war, battle, fight

πολεμόω: to make hostile, make an enemy (also in mid.)

πολιορκέω: to beseige, form a blockade

πολιορκία, ἡ: a siege, blockade

πόλις, εως, ἡ: a city-state, city

πολλάκις: many times, often, frequently

πολύς, πολλά, πολύ: much, many

πόνος, ὁ: work, toil

ποτέ: ever, at some time, once

που: anywhere, somewhere; I suppose

πράσσω: to do, accomplish, make, act

πρέσβυς, εως, ὁ: old, old (man); ambassador, envoy

πρίν: until, before

πρό: before, in front, of, in place of (gen.)

προ-δίδωμι: to betray, give over

προ-δοσία, ἡ: betrayal, treason, giving up

προ-έχω: to hold forth; be first, surpass, excel

προ-καλέω: to call forth; propose or offer; (mostly mid.) provoke, challenge

πρό-οπτος, ον: foreseen, manifest

προ-οράω: to see beforehand; see before one's eyes; take thought of

πρός: to (acc.), near, in addition to (dat.)

προσ-βάλλω: to attack, strike against, dash

πρόσ-ειμι (εἰμί): to be in addition, be added to; to be present

προσ-ήκω: to have come, be present; to be fitting or proper; to belong to, concern

προσ-λαμβάνω: to take in addition

προσ-φέρω: to bring upon, deal with attack

πρῶτος, η, ον: first, early

Πύλος, ου, ἡ: Pylos, a city in the
    Peloponnese
πώποτε: yet ever, ever
πῶς: how? in what way?

Ρ

ῥῆμα, ατος, τό: word, saying, speech
ῥῆσις, εως, ἡ: a saying, speech
ῥοπή, ἡ: weighing or turn (of a scale);
    weight

Σ

σαφής, ές: clear, distinct, definite
σῖτος, ὁ: grain, bread, food
σκοπέω: to look at, examine, consider
σπονδή, ἡ: a drink-offering; truce, treaty
στράτευμα, τό: an expedition,
    campaign, army
στρατεύω: to march, campaign
στρατηγός, ὁ: general
στρατία, ἡ: an army, expedition, land
    force
στρατοπεδεύω: to encamp, take a
    position
στρατός, τό: army, encamped army
σφάλλω: to make fall, overthrow, defeat;
    frustrate; (pass.) be overthrown; go
    wrong, be frustrated, be mistaken in
    something (gen.)
σφεῖς: they
σφέτερος, η, ον: their own, their
σῴζω: to save, keep, preserve
σωτηρία, ἡ: deliverance, safety
σώφρων, ον: prudent, moderate

Τ

τε: and, both
Τεισίας, ὁ: Teisias
Τεισίμαχος, ὁ: Teisimachus
τελευτάω: to end, complete, finish; die

τελευτή, ἡ: an end, completion, out-
    come; death
τίθημι: to set, put, place, arrange
τιμωρία, ἡ: punishment; help, aid
τις, τι: anyone, -thing; someone, -thing
τίς, τί: who? which?
τοίνυν: well then; therefore, accordingly
τοιόσδε, άδε, όνδε: such
τοιοῦτος, -αύτη, -οῦτο: such
τολμάω: to dare, undertake, endure
τοξότης, ὁ: an archer, bowman
τοσοῦτος, -αύτη, -οῦτο: so (or such)
    great, so many, so much
τρέπω: to turn, direct
τριάκοντα: thirty
τριακόσιοι, αι, α: three hundred
τρόπος, ὁ: a manner, way; turn, direction
τυγχάνω: to chance upon, get; happen
τύχη, ἡ: chance, luck, fortune, success

Υ

ὑμεῖς: you
ὑμέτερος, α, ον: your, yours
ὑπ-ακούω: to heed, listen to (gen.);
    to yield (to), submit (to), comply
    (with) (dat.)
ὑπ-άρχω: to be there, exist, be ready, be
    available
ὑπ-ήκοος, ον: heeding, obeying; being
    subject to
ὑπό: by, because of, from (gen.); under
    (dat.)
ὑπο-λαμβάνω: to take up, reply;
    interrupt; suppose
ὑπό-νοια, ἡ: suspicion, notion, thought
ὑπ-οπτεύω: to suspect, hold in suspicion
ὕπ-οπτος, ον: to viewed with suspicion

ὑπο-τελής, ἐς: tributary, subject to
  tribute or taxes
ὑπο-τίθημι: to place under, advise,
  propose
ὕστερος, α, ον: later, last

Φ

φαίνομαι: to appear, seem; to become
  visible, be seen
φανερός, ά, όν: visible, manifest,
  evident
φέρω: to bear, carry, bring, convey
φημί: to say, claim, assert
φιλία, ἡ: friendship, affection, love
Φιλοκράτης, ὁ: Philocrates
φιλονικέω: to be fond of victory,
  contentious; obstinate
φίλος, η, ον: friendly; (subst.) friend, kin
Φλειάσιος, α, ον: Phliasian
φοβέω: to put to flight, terrify, frighten
φόβος, ὁ: fear, terror, panic
φρονέω: to think, to have (particular
  kinds of) thoughts; to be wise, prudent;
  to agree
φυγάς, άδος, ὁ: fugitive, an exile
φυλακή, ἡ: a guard, watch, garrison
φυλάσσω: to guard; (mid.) to guard
  against
φύσις, εως, ἡ: nature, character

Χ–Ψ

χαλεπός, ά, όν: difficult, hard, harmful
χειμών, ῶνος τό: storm, winter
χειρόω: to subdue, master
χείρων, ον: worse, inferior
χίλιοι, αι, α: thousand
Χίος, α, ον: Chian, of Chios (island)
χράομαι: to use, employ, engage in (dat.)

χρήσιμος, η, ον: good, useful,
  serviceable
χρησμος, ὁ: oracle, oracular response
χρόνος, ὁ: time
χωρίον, τό: place, spot, region
ψέγω: blame, censure, find fault with

Ω

ὡς: as, thus, so, that; when, since
ὥσπερ: as, just as, as if
ὥστε: so that, that, so as to; and so
ὠφελέω: to benefit, help; be profitable
ὠφελία, ἡ: benefit, help
ὠφέλιμος, α, ον: useful, beneficial